Why Her?

YOU, YOUR MOTHER-IN-LAW,
and the BIG PICTURE

LISA HUNTER, RHONDA HUNTER,
AND ELIZABETH HUNTER

Acknowledgments

I could not have written a single thought down on these pages if it weren't for God's guidance. I am grateful to You, God, for that and for so much more. Thank You for blessing me with an incredible husband, who encouraged me throughout this project.

Josh, I can't thank you enough for all the hours you spent listening to me and helping me to process my thoughts. I know that half the time, you had no idea what I was trying to say because, as John Gray so aptly noted, "men are from Mars, and women are from Venus," but you listened anyway and kept me going with your encouragement. I love you so much, and I'm so thankful that I get to spend every day with you. I am honored to be your wife.

Thanks go to my amazing children, Noah and Ava. Noah, what a gift you are to your dad and me. God gave us the perfect son when He blessed us with you. We are in awe of the man that God is molding you into. Your love for Jesus, your compassionate heart, and the way you love and care for others continue to inspire us to be better people. You are the best son and the best big brother that anyone could ever ask for. I love you, buddy, and I am honored to be your mom! Ava, what a gift you are to your dad and me. God gave us the perfect little girl when He blessed us with you. We are in awe of the way God has used and continues to use your five years that were on this earth to make a difference and build His kingdom. Your love for Jesus, zest for life, and giant-like courage and strength continue to inspire Daddy and me to be better people. You are the best daughter and the best sister anyone could ever ask for. I love you, baby girl, and I am honored to be your mommy!

I'm thankful to Patty Gable, my mom, who helped me get to know Jesus when I was a young girl. Your encouragement regarding the book and the time you spent with my children throughout the writing process were great gifts to me. I am grateful to you, Mom, for that and so much more.

I'm thankful for so many friends at Northland and Summit Churches and RDV Sportsplex who helped me think through what might be helpful to daughters-in-law who pick up this book. I am grateful to each one of you for that and so much more.

I am thankful for two wonderful sisters-in-law. Rhonda and Lizzy, you are simply the best, and doing this project with you in order to encourage the women who will read it was a fun challenge. I am grateful to you for that and so much more.

I want to thank my mother- and father-in-law, Becky and Joel Hunter, for raising an incredible, godly son for me to marry, and for praying for "Josh's wife" before you ever met me. I am grateful to you for that and for so much more.

Last, but not least, I want to thank you, the reader, for inspiring me to share my thoughts on the important mother-in-law/daughter-in-law relationship so that you might be encouraged to love your mother-in-law well. I am grateful for you.

—Lisa Hunter

First, I want to thank God for the grace He has shown in my life. I count it an amazing privilege that He uses me, a fallen person, to do work for His kingdom.

To my parents, Kim and Ron Hauser, thank you for teaching me about that grace as a little girl. Thank you for instilling confidence in me, letting me know that Jesus loves me. Thanks for helping me to understand how to leverage God's blessings in my life in order to bless others. I am grateful for your steadfast prayers, which included petitions for me to have a godly husband and in-laws who love Jesus and each other. Thank you for being the remarkable grandparents that you are. I couldn't have taken on this project without all your help with the kids. They love you like crazy, and so do I.

I thank Kelly Hauser, my sister and best friend, for her help with the daughter-in-law perspective of this book and for helping me to decide what to include in these chapters. Kelly, you, more than anyone I know, cherish others. I don't know what my life would look like without you in it.

I also want to thank Tiffany Hauser, my sister-in-law. You are the perfect daughter-in-law. Thank you for being such a blessing to my brother and our entire family.

To Matthew Hauser, my brother, thank you for your encouragement during the writing and for the much-needed vacation for our family.

Ashli Evans, one of my dearest friends, life would not be nearly as fun without you. Thank you for letting me process ideas with you. And thanks for your editing help with my chapters. For as long as I have known you, you have been the perfect example of a wife, mother, and daughter-in-law who keeps the "big picture" in mind.

Kelsey Christmas, my sweet friend, thank you for letting me bounce ideas off you during our walks and for giving me very real, godly advice. Thanks, too, for watching my kids when I needed more time to write. Your excitement for life and love for Jesus are contagious.

Allison Adams, the most amazing executive assistant and friend, thank you for all of your help with our family's scheduling and correspondence. Thank you for praying for us. You keep our family running smoothly.

Brandy Parker, I can't do anything ministry-related without being extremely grateful to you. I am so thankful that God prompted both your heart and John's to start Summit Church alongside Isaac and me. It has been such a fun journey.

To my Summit Connect Group, the Summit Church staff, and their sweet families, I love serving Jesus alongside you. Thank you for praying for me as I wrote, offering helpful advice, and being open about your personal experiences with your in-laws. You all do such an amazing job helping people understand they matter to God.

Lizzy and Lisa Hunter, you two made this project so fun. I couldn't ask for two better sisters-in-law.

To Becky and Joel Hunter, my in-laws, you are two of the biggest blessings in my life. Thank you for praying for me before you ever knew me. Thank you for raising an amazing son who really loves Jesus. Thanks for being wonderful grandparents. Mom, your wisdom and perseverance always astound me. I know this book would have been much easier for you if it had been a solo endeavor, but I am grateful I got to be part of it.

Thanks go to my daughter Jada, who has been as excited as I have been about this book. Thanks for reading my chapters and for reminding me of funny family stories. The way you think, the way you process, will be a blessing to others throughout your lifetime.

Thanks go to my daughter Ella for her many book cover "drawings" and for help with my outfit choices for the author pictures. I know God is going to use your creative eye for something awesome.

And thanks go to Lincoln, my son. Thanks for making Mommy laugh with your funny stories. I can't wait to see how God will use your ability to tell a great story in the future.

Finally, thanks to Isaac Hunter, my sweet husband and partner in ministry, and a fantastic dad to our children. I couldn't have done any of this without you. Thank you for helping my ideas and writing make sense. Thank you for staying awake with me while I tried to make late-night deadlines. But thank you most of all for giving me a life filled with awesome adventures and purpose much greater than us. I love you.

—Rhonda Hunter

This book was a combined effort by so many people, whose insights, wisdom, and talents shaped these chapters. I am grateful to God for blessing me with this opportunity to partner with my wonderful family on this project.

I thank my mother-in-law, Becky. Thank you for including us in your vision. Thank you for inspiring me through your love for Jesus, which bleeds over into every facet of your relationship with me. Watching you and Pop live what you say has shaped my life in innumerable ways. Thank you for praying for me even before you knew me. Thank you for gently leading Lisa, Rhonda, and me through this process and for encouraging us every step of the way. I am blessed beyond words to be your daughter-in-law.

To José and Shirley Ariza, my incredible parents, I love you so much. Thank you for your unconditional love. Thank you for teaching me about Jesus and imparting godly wisdom into every aspect of my life. Thank you for allowing me to write about your life experiences that provide invaluable insights. Thank you for the entertaining life that you've given me, which inspired many an illustration.

Thanks go to my dear sister-in-law and friend, Kaci Ariza, for allowing me to pick her brain repeatedly throughout this undertaking. You are such a blessing to me.

Thanks also go to Bill and Barbara Peterson for being such shining examples of incredible in-laws for my brother. I value you so much as family.

My gratitude goes to my friend Kari Rodriguez. You have been an amazing help through this process. Your words of wisdom and your life experiences have had a profound impact on this manuscript. Thank you, dear friend.

Special thanks go to Maggie Popp and Kate Jacobsen. It was a huge blessing to get to do life with you while we lived in Kansas during Joel's fellowship year and my writing of this book. Thank you for adding insight to this process. You are inspirational women.

Rhonda and Lisa Hunter, I love being your sister-in-law. You made this process such a wonderful experience. I love you girls.

Luke Hunter, you are the apple of my eye. You inspire me in more ways than you will ever know. I love you, son.

To my best friend and my hero, Joel Hunter, I can't believe I get to be your wife. Thank you for supporting me through this process. Thank you for your encouragement, your patience, and your prayers. Thank you for lending your editing eye to this project. You make me so much better than I am on my own. I love you.

—Elizabeth Hunter

Our sincere appreciation goes to Melissa Bogdany for her professional edits, to Tracy Weiss for the layout and cover design, to Dede Caruso for additional formatting and to Robert Andrescik for his encouragement and professional assistance in the publishing phase of this project.

And a big thank you to Josh Hunter and Kellie Harding for the authors' cover photographs and to Jolie Duncan for using her cosmetic talents to get us picture ready.

—Lisa, Rhonda, and Elizabeth Hunter

Why Her?

YOU, YOUR MOTHER-IN-LAW,
and the BIG PICTURE

LISA HUNTER, RHONDA HUNTER,
AND ELIZABETH HUNTER

WHY HER? You, Your Mother-in-Law, and the Big Picture
by Lisa Hunter, Rhonda Hunter and Elizabeth Hunter

ISBN 978-0-9786783-3-3

Printed in the United States of America

Dedication

We dedicate this book to the women who will one day be our daughters-in-law: Mrs. Noah Hunter, Mrs. Lincoln Hunter, and Mrs. Luke Hunter, as well as the wives of any sons who may be born to us in the future. We have been praying for each of you since the days our sons were born, and we will never stop. May you be blessed and be a blessing.

Contents

Introduction

IF YOU'VE PICKED up this book in a bookstore, you're probably a mother-in-law, or a daughter-in-law, or a husband who's trying to get his wife to notice him reading the book in order to draw her interest without offending her. If you have received this book as a gift, it probably has little to do with your culinary abilities or your child-rearing skills. Whoever gave you this book probably has a genuine desire for you to have the most fruitful relationship possible with your mother-in-law. If you read that last sentence and rolled your eyes, this book is for you.

As three sisters-in-law, one of the biggest blessings in our lives is the relationship we have with our mother-in-law, Becky. The fruit from that relationship was the catalyst for this book. Inspired by our mother-in-law's vision, we decided to join together on the project of sharing our experience as daughters-in-law with those whom it may benefit.

Your relationship may be a cold war or may look more like a Switzerland and (insert any country here). Whether you desire simply to kill the tension or to take your relationship from a stagnant state to a more congenial situation, we are confident this book will be of great use. We wanted our blessing to bless others. Hopefully, this book will inspire you to keep that towel you were thinking of throwing in, and give your relationship with your mother-in-law another go. We know from experience that it is definitely worth it.

Chapter One

Connect Two Families

—Elizabeth Hunter

G ENERALLY WHEN WE hear the term "mother-in-law," we think of a stereotypical sitcom caricature, the outspoken mom who drops by unannounced to criticize your child-rearing, insult your interior design abilities, and supply your husband with the nourishment that your cooking inadequacies prevent you from providing him. Rarely do we consider that the relationship between our husbands' mothers and us can step beyond mere civility and be one of the most meaningful relationships of our lives.

Do You Take This Man ... and His Mother?

Love is patient, love is kind. It does not envy, it does not boast,
it is not proud. It is not rude, it is not self-seeking,
it is not easily angered, it keeps no record of wrongs.
1 CORINTHIANS 13:4-5 NIV

With so much to take into consideration on a wedding day, what lies at the forefront of a bride's mind? When you think about your wedding day—that "big day" that warrants the dedication of entire magazines, books, and websites—what was most important to you? If you are like me, an honest response might be, "What wasn't on my mind? I focused on everything."

It all matters to us—the invitations and the flowers and that candlelight-colored dress that we dreamed of wearing since we were little girls. (Really, it was white in our dreams, but at the time, we didn't know that candlelight was a color and not just a noun.) Only now do we realize how much better it looks than white with our skin tones, so despite the fact that our mothers say "people talk" if a bride doesn't wear white, we seriously consider it. And then we turn our thoughts to the most monumental strut of our lives down the wide center aisle, and are startled to realize that the church of our childhood has two side aisles only. So we mentally prepare ourselves to process down one side and recess up the other. Oh, sure, there is the option of holding the wedding outdoors, but who can predict the weather? And one drop of rain can make a bride's hair particularly attractive to a variety of winged creatures for nesting and offspring-rearing purposes.

Will the caterers remember that your uncle has a shellfish allergy? Will the DJ remember no chicken dance? The electric slide is all right, but definitely no chicken dance. And a conga line—that's okay, too. It's a universal sign that people are having fun. How are you going to keep your granny from going out with the single ladies to catch the bouquet? Who's going to keep your cousin from doing that thing where he lights cocktail napkins on fire with tea candles? Will someone remember to grab your change of shoes from the church? Will they take the fondant off the wedding cake before serving it? They need to take the fondant off the wedding cake! And what is fondant, anyway?

In the rigorous planning of the biggest celebration of our lives, while focusing on 7,000 details, we may not have thought about what we were gaining beyond the man of our dreams—oh, and the fondue set that we registered for (who can enter into married life without one?) and that requisite re-gifted crystal cat figurine (nothing is more celebratory, I assure you). In addition to our shiny new slow cookers, we may not have considered that we are inheriting shiny new family members.

New relatives, some of them particularly significant, enter our lives that day, and we need to take them for better or for worse, not only during holidays, but also when they feel like popping in, as friends or as food critics. More than likely, we were not considering our mothers-in-law as we took the great plunge into marriage. Whether your relationship with your mother-in-law is new, or has long since lost its newness, consider a few thoughts:

1. Who is this woman?

If you think of your mother-in-law only as the person who questioned your virtue when you decided to wear pink shoes under your wedding gown, or can only picture her as the woman whose unexpected visits send you into a frenzy of closing blinds and turning off lights to convince her you're not home, maybe it's time to consider her from a new perspective.

We do have something in common with our mothers-in-law. We love our husbands, and our mothers-in-law love them, too. The choices we make and actions we take regarding our mothers-in-law need to reflect this seemingly simple, yet immeasurably important, fact.

> We love our husbands, and our mothers-in-law love them, too.

You know, there is a real possibility that when your mother-in-law watched you walk down that side aisle toward her son, she wasn't thinking about ways she could make your life difficult. She may have been watching the fruition of all her efforts and ambitions in raising that man who was holding your hand at the altar. Our mothers-in-law spent years upon years pouring themselves into the men that we love so well. What we love most about our husbands may be the direct result of persistent efforts by their mothers. It is good for us to keep in mind that they have given us gifts in the men who made us want to say, "I do." Remembering that our mothers-in-law are moms can help us have a better perspective on who they are. Most of us already know how to love a mom well.

2. Why does she act this way?

In a single wedding day, a groom transforms from a boy who looks to his mother for help to a man responsible for his own family. That leap is probably as difficult for our mothers-in-law to make as it is for our husbands. So as we feel frustration toward these women, let's consider more than their words or actions; let's consider their motivations as we choose how to respond. What may seem to be malicious or meddling may be neither. They just may be trying to care for their sons. Considering their motivation reminds us of that significant thing we have in common—him.

This may not necessarily remove every frustration caused by mothers-in-law's actions, but at least it will provide some insight that can be a good starting point to help us choose our best response to them. When it comes down to it, actions are a result of choice. Although we can't control other people's behavior, we do have the benefit of choosing how we will respond.

3. What can I do?

Instead of being reactive to frustrating situations, there are steps we can take to be proactive. It is rare that any human being will respond poorly to active kindness. We may feel like our mothers-in-law are grappling to keep their sons instead of embracing us as daughters who are now part of the families. There are ways we can begin to instill confidence in our mothers-in-law. Living in a way that helps them sense their families are expanding, not dividing, is possible.

At the wedding of a dear friend of mine, Kari Rodriguez, I saw a precious example of how a daughter-in-law can honor her new mom-in-law. Kari used that day to pay tribute to her husband's mother. Not only did she prevent barriers between her mother-in-law and herself that day, but she also created an environment that made it unlikely for a barrier to ever go up between them.

Kari's husband, Ray, had lost his father several years before their wedding. His father had been Ray's best friend and Ray's mother's lifelong love. Although he was not there in person, Kari made sure his memory was a focal point of the day. While in the planning stages, Kari consulted with Ray and her soon-to-be mother-in-law and chose Ray's father's birthday as the date for the wedding. During the reception, an announcement was made about the significance of the wedding date. A place was set next to Kari's mother-in-law for her late husband, and a picture of him and a candle were placed there in his honor. Kari also chose a special song to be played for Ray and his mother that depicted their relationship. Kari's new mother-in-law was definitely recognized and embraced by her son's very thoughtful wife.

Although many brides view a wedding as their big day or the day they have been dreaming about since childhood, it's helpful to have a bigger perspective on what is being celebrated among the flowers and the string trio and the beef or chicken. Merriam-Webster has an apt definition of marriage: "an act, process, or instance of joining in close association." The wedding day is a day to celebrate the joining of a husband and wife. The celebration also can honor the connection of a bride and groom to their new families. What a great opportunity to start a new life, as my friend Kari did, remembering that this day is not only about the girl in the white (or candlelight) dress and veil, but is about celebrating family. Whether your wedding is in the planning stages or has long since passed, you will have opportunities to be frustrated with your mother-in-law. But whether it is your wedding day or another day, don't allow frustrations to determine the tone of your relationship with her. Remember the reason you had a wedding. You got to marry the man you love more than any other. And part of loving him well is being good to a mother who loves him too.

Consider a mother-in-law's point of view:
It meant so much to me that my daughter-in-law began including me as family when she began planning the wedding. She invited me to look at dresses then, and even today she makes a real effort to include me in her life.

Be the daughter-in-law you would like to have:
- Make a decision to show kindness to your mother-in-law. Do something to honor her.
- Set the tone for your relationship with her; be proactive and respond reasonably, even when she frustrates you.
- Pray for a perspective of your mother-in-law that is not limited solely to your personal interactions with her. She raised your husband, that man that you love so dearly.

> *"I dreamed of a wedding of elaborate elegance, a church filled with family and friends. I asked him what kind of wedding he wished for, and he said one that would make me his wife."*
> —Anonymous

Tradition: Rewarding Ritual or Rigid Requirement?

*Do nothing out of selfish ambition or vain conceit, but in humility consider
others better than yourselves. Each of you should look not only
to your own interests, but also to the interests of others.*
PHILIPPIANS 2:3-4 NIV

All families have traditions, some conventional, others, less so. Some bring a smile to our faces; attending Christmas Eve candlelight services with the whole family. Some bring a less delighted expression to our faces; the annual Thanksgiving fight between my father and my brothers over who gets to eat the turkey heart. Unappealing as that ritual is, without it and the winsome backdrop of the Macy's parade, Thanksgiving would be just another Thursday to my family.

As your family expands and you merge with your husband's, the matriarch of his family, your mother-in-law, is bound to bring some of her own family traditions into the mix. As lots of new traditions get combined with old ones, it feels much like a to-do list. It may feel like your husband's mother is putting pressure on you to uphold all of their traditions, or you simply may be assuming she would want you to keep their traditions and you are the one putting pressure on yourself. A sense of obligation can easily result in undue stress and frustration, which is certainly unhelpful in relationship building. As we sift through the piles of rituals that two connected families bring to the table, it is important to keep in mind the goal of upholding traditions.

"Tradition" comes from a Latin word, traditio, which means "the action of handing over." The object is to unite families and immerse our children and our children's children in rich culture and a sense of heritage. What is it you want to hand over to your children—a litany of legalistic requirements concerning family celebrations, or encouragement to celebrate family being together whenever there is an occasion to gather?

As I was running errands on a breezy, moderately warm day in September, I was reminded of one of my traditions. I went into a store, and to my delight, they were already selling Christmas decorations. It may have been an inappropriately long way off, but it reminded me of what was waiting around the corner. (Okay, a couple of corners, considering there are still several significant holidays occurring prior to December 25. Actually, depending on whether you observe either Leif Erikson Day or Guy Fawkes Day, you may be completing a parallelogram.) As the holidays approach (Thanksgiving and Christmas, not those celebrating Leif or Guy), I begin preparing for my husband's least favorite tradition of mine: my late-night pre-holiday pie-baking session. It always starts the same way:

Joel: Where are you going?
Me: To the store. I have to get stuff to make pies.
Joel: Are you really going to make pies? Why don't you just buy a pie?
Me: No, I always make pies. I love making pies!
Joel: I'm not sure you do. You always get so stressed.
Me: You get stressed. I love to bake!

Fast forward to 2 A.M. Everything in the kitchen is sticky and covered with flour. The dog looks like I tried to cover her with paper-mâché, and I am left with several mediocre-tasting pies with chewy crusts. (Why can I not master pie crusts?) Then, since I have stayed up so late, I am exhausted the next day and can't enjoy the time I have to celebrate the holiday with my loved ones. Annually, it becomes clear in hindsight that I could have taken a great deal of stress out of the occasion by prioritizing quality time with my family over an abnormal, irrepressible desire to bake pies from scratch. Decades from now, I will never remember that I didn't bake a pie on a particular Thanksgiving, but I will remember that I generally felt tired to the point of nausea every year we gathered around the banquet table. I should have just bought a pie and dumped a bag of flour on the floor. I would have achieved a better outcome. (Honey, you were right.)

A realization like this leads to a really important question that can have a big impact on your relationship with your mother-in-law: What traditions are you upholding simply for the sake of doing what your family has done in the past and not for the sake of building the relationship with your current family? What traditions of your husband's and your mother-in-law's might you be throwing out because they won't leave room for your own traditions? It makes the decision whether to keep a tradition easier when we measure the value of that tradition by its end result.

In my previous example, the end result of my traditional pie-baking neurosis is so-so pies, a mess in the kitchen, and an unpleasant holiday with my family because I have exhausted myself to the point of dysfunction. Perhaps it is time to give up the ghost and choose a tradition that is focused on spending more time with my husband and family and spending less time cleaning the kitchen and bathing the dog.

Take a look at some of your mother-in-law's traditions. Before dismissing them simply because they haven't been your own, consider that not only might she feel honored if you adopt them, but your husband and family might love them. You may not be keen on the idea of having venison fondue every Christmas Eve, but if it brings the people you care about around the table for some quality time, it may soften you toward the idea. And maybe the rest of your family would just love it. Mine would. It would be a great culinary leap above turkey hearts.

If you are faced with a mother-in-law who is quite pushy when it comes to her traditions, sit down with her and discuss options. Because you hold the role of daughter-in-law doesn't mean you can't hold an eye-to-eye conversation. You are both adults, and there's a better chance she'll respect your wishes if she knows what they are. And even if you aren't picking up on a tone of respect from her, life would be easier for you and your husband if you remained calm and levelheaded. You can respect her as a person and listen to her opinions without agreeing with everything she says and without being obligated to do whatever she hopes you will do.

Choose your response—and your tone—wisely, and don't allow your passion about a particular Easter menu item or birthday celebration format to dictate your behavior. If you deliberately value your relationships with your new family more than the familiar traditions you are comfortable with, chances are you will be able to reach a compromise that will do honor to both.

Consider a mother-in-law's point of view:

"I think mothers-in-law need to keep more things to themselves and daughters-in-law should just be themselves," says Shirley Ariza, my mom and veteran mother-in-law. Gentle honesty is one thing that is never underappreciated in a good mother-in-law/daughter-in-law relationship. Gentle honesty doesn't step on toes, and it can prevent lots of future frustration.

Be the daughter-in-law you would like to have:
- Remember the goal of your traditions is to bring your family closer. It may be time to let the stressful ones go.
- Consider your mother-in-law's traditions thoughtfully. Your family might love them, and you will honor her by including them.
- Be open to the possibility of developing brand new traditions together. It may be a good way to have a fresh start and initiate bonding.
- Pray, and then sit down and talk to your mother-in-law if the two of you are locking horns on a subject. Stresses in your relationship with her are about more than you or her; the greater good of your family is the bigger concern.

"Tradition simply means that we need to end what began well
and continue what is worth continuing."
—JOSE BERGAMIN

Choose How You'll Celebrate Holidays

"Martha, Martha," the Lord answered, "you are worried and upset
about many things, but only one thing is needed.
Mary has chosen what is better, and it will not be taken away from her."
LUKE 10:41-42 NIV

Ah, the holidays . . . the occasions that bring us together with our nearest and dearest to celebrate through various forms of eating, drinking, and merriment—or, all too often, through arguing, awkward tension, and turkey heart consumption (see previous section on traditions).

The holidays should be a time focused on enjoying family, a time to commemorate momentous or miraculous events. All too often, though, we seem to lose sight of the spirit of a holiday and dive into a struggle for possession of it. Unfortunately, it's not unusual for women to fall victim to this attitude. "I ALWAYS host Thanksgiving." Or, "I ALWAYS make Easter brunch." Or, "I

ALWAYS bring the 'eh' pies with the really chewy bottom crusts." (Seriously, why does that happen? I chill the dough. I don't overwork it. Still, they're always chewy.)

As we merge our families with our husbands', often we enter into stalemates over who gets which holiday at which time with which menu assignment. In order to meet everyone's desires and expectations, you may feel you have to compromise your idea of a traditional holiday beyond your comfort level.

When my husband, Joel, joined my family for our first Christmas together, he was surprised at how different our celebration was from the ones he'd had in his family. He had never seen people put candles on a cake and sing "Happy Birthday" to Jesus before exchanging gifts, but I didn't realize that this wasn't a common Christmas morning practice. Nor did I realize that it wasn't usual for dads to receive bratwursts in their Christmas stockings each year. My dad always did. I guess my mom knew he just really liked brats. I'm not sure how she kept them fresh. Ice packs, I suppose. Or Christmas magic.

On Joel's second Christmas with my family, he was prepared for the annual singing of the birthday song. He gladly joined in, welcoming this new tradition into his own life. Feeling settled into the way my family celebrates Christmas, he didn't expect to be thrown any curve balls. Unfortunately for Joel, my family is big on surprises—oftentimes with complete disregard for propriety. This particular Christmas my family and I had combined our budget for Joel's gifts and purchased him something we knew he really wanted but didn't at all expect to receive. Instead of just giving him the gift and allowing the wrapping paper to confer the element of surprise, my father decided it would be better to wrap the gift, then hide it, and complete the transaction by giving Joel a poem written by Santa Claus that told him where to search for it.

My father asked Joel to read the poem aloud for everyone to hear. And since Santa Claus is from Washington Heights, the poem was written in a New York dialect. Here is Santa's poem that Joel read aloud in front of my entire family:

I knows yuz aint got no belief in me
So I aint left yuz nottin undah da tree
But diss aint no jip
I done wan yuz ta flip
Cause behind da couch daiz is somtin ta see
Luv,
Santiclaus an dem shawt little elves

This certainly was not Joel's idea of a traditional family Christmas. His parents never had him read aloud poems from Santa Claus in order to locate his presents. And I'm fairly certain that they still don't know Santa Claus is a New Yorker. Joel didn't follow the traditions of a Hunter family Christmas, but a new way of approaching Christmas in no way diminished it for him. It was still the celebration of the birth of Christ, just honoring Him through a little more sweat and a little more singing.

As you are deciding how to celebrate holidays, remember that the reason for celebration is the same whether you stay at your own house or dine at your mother-in-law's. The reason will be the same whether you make your sweet potato casserole with marshmallows on top or she makes her "more refined" version sans Jet-Puffed. And the reason will be the same whether you burn the midnight oil baking pies or she brings hers, with their highly overrated flaky crusts.

The particulars of a holiday don't have to become sticking points if we decide not to become too particular. Again, having a rational conversation with your mother-in-law, one in which you really listen to what she's saying and prayerfully respond to her, can be the quickest way to solving what may at first appear to be irresolvable conflicts. Workable solutions end up looking different for every family. Each family is unique, so why wouldn't solutions to families' relationship issues be unique, too? All that matters is that they work.

There are lots of ways to make holidays more enjoyable. My sister-in-law Kaci has wonderful parents who have always been gracious hosts to my parents (Kaci's in-laws). Instead of having my brother, Daniel, and her wear out trying to race between their families on special days, her parents, Barbara and Bill, invite my parents, my siblings, and my family to their home, and we all celebrate together. My friend Maggie's family lives too far from her in-laws to get everyone together, so she and her husband split the holiday weekend and spend part with her family and part with her husband's. My mother's mother and my mother's mother-in-law both lived in a state that was miles away from her. She flew her mother down one year for Christmas and her mother-in-law the next, alternating their visits for years.

I have been blessed with a very accommodating mother-in-law. Every Thanksgiving, instead of celebrating with their children and their children's families on Thanksgiving Day, she and my father-in-law celebrate with us another day during that week. That is one of my favorite parts of the holiday, going over to Mom and Pop's to spend time with my husband's family. It's no less Thanksgiving because it isn't Thursday. In fact, it would feel less like Thanksgiving without this time together. The emphasis is not on a date or a time. The emphasis is on bringing the family together. That's certainly the best way I can think to celebrate.

Consider a mother-in-law's point of view:

I appreciate how accommodating my daughter-in-law is. She asks about our schedules and gives us her family's schedule as well so that we can not only coordinate occasional activities, but also be specific in our prayers for each other. It is wonderful that she always makes an effort to let me know that she likes time with me and makes an effort to see that it happens.

Be the daughter-in-law you would like to have:

- Remain open-minded about the way you celebrate holidays. A new way of celebrating doesn't diminish the reason for the celebration.
- If menu items are causing tension, draw assignments out of a hat while the family is together, so each person knows what he or she is to bring for the next family get-together.
- Alternate visits with your family and your husband's on holidays. Try giving time to your family on Thanksgiving and taking time with your husband's on Christmas, then switch the next year.
- Bring both families together to celebrate if your family and your husband's family live within close enough proximity and you can find a place to make that work.
- Pray, and then have a rational, loving conversation with your mother-in-law if you are in a stalemate about plans for a particular event. Determine the best solution; consider compromising, cooperating, or alternating between her preference and yours.

"One man's ways may be as good as another's, but we all like our own best."
—JANE AUSTEN

Chapter Two

Love Your Mother-in-Law's Son

—Rhonda Hunter

THIS COMPONENT ALONE may not make your relationship with your mother-in-law, but it can break it. Even if you get everything else wrong, if you get this right, you and your mother-in-law will have enough for a relationship. Your man is the boy she raised from birth. She wants you to treat him well.

One night, I was rocking my two-year-old son before I put him down to sleep. His warm little body leaned against mine, his tiny little hand clasped my necklace, and an overwhelming sense of love for him came over me. It occurred to me that just a few short decades ago, my mother-in-law rocked her sons when they were my son's age. She loved them like I love my son.

I pray all the time that my little boy will one day marry just the right girl, that they love each other well and honor God in their marriage. My mother-in-law loved my husband like I love my son; she prayed for him like I pray for mine. Now, God has given me the opportunity to be, and the responsibility of being, an answer to her prayers.

In his "iMarriage" series, Pastor Andy Stanley described loving your spouse well like this: "God wants to use you as the primary means by which His unconditional love is expressed in a human relationship." That is a pretty huge responsibility! So, if we are going to carry out our roles well, we are going to need God's help, and we must be willing to offer our whole being: body, mind, and soul.

Love Him With Your Body

Do you not know that your bodies are temples of the Holy Spirit,
who is in you, whom you have received from God? You are not your own;
you were bought at a price. Therefore honor God with your bodies.
1 CORINTHIANS 6:19-20 NIV

I know what you are thinking: This section is going to be about sex. No, it's not! I can assure you that my mother-in-law would rather die than picture me in bed with her son. So I'll spare all of us the embarrassment of opening up a conversation that neither you, nor I ever wanted to have with our mothers, let alone our husbands' mothers. I will say this, though: Sex is an important part of marriage. God created it for a husband and wife to enjoy. Enjoy it!

I want to use this time with you to encourage you to take care of yourself, in part, so that you can better care for your husband. There are multiple benefits to physical wellbeing. When you make an effort to feel good and look nice, your husband is blessed. When you bless him, you add to your mother-in-law's reasons to be grateful for you.

When people talk about the importance of health and wellness, they tend either to idolize it beyond the point that is helpful, or marginalize it, as if it is only a legitimate issue for non-spiritual people who care merely about physical things. To err on either side is unwise. Paul himself spoke of physical training as being of "some value" (1 Timothy 4:8).

I think we can all agree on two things. The first is that we feel better when we eat fairly healthily and get a little exercise. Doing those things is a matter of discipline and perseverance. It is little right choices, every day. Our physical bodies affect our moods, our outlooks, our temperaments, and so on. We are human so if we ignore our physical needs, we do so at our own peril and our spouses', too.

Every now and then, it is good to ask ourselves the question "Would I want to come home to me?" There may be times when, if we are honest with ourselves, we have to answer our question with a no. We all have off days when we can't seem to pull it together. But if our answer is consistently negative, we may need to change some habits, because the fact of the matter is, people are coming home to us, and we hope they are looking forward to seeing us.

The second thing I think we can agree on is this: There was a reason your husband was attracted to you in the first place. No doubt, you have a dynamic personality and great charisma, but something tells me he was attracted to the way you looked and carried yourself, too. Men are visual creatures. After we get married and our husbands have seen us not looking our best, it gets easier and easier for us to justify slacking off and never bothering to pull ourselves together for our husbands. In fact, it's easy to get to the point where we only try hard to look attractive when we are around other people. Our husbands may be there, too, but we aren't trying to impress him. He is an afterthought.

Trying to remain attractive is no easy task. It takes effort to look nice. If you have little kids and have the privilege of staying home with them, it may be even harder. Taking a shower and blow-drying your hair can seem like a waste of time because you know you are going to be spit up on the minute you put on clean clothing. But your husband has been at work all day with other women who have showered and smell good. I'm guessing he would appreciate coming home to a wife who has at least tried to clean herself up.

A little exercise benefits you in numerous ways, too. You release endorphins. You feel more attractive. You carry yourself with more confidence. A confident woman is always more attractive than an insecure one. It might be one of the only things you accomplish in your day with little ones around, but it will make a big difference in the long run for your family if you put some effort into your physical health and wellness.

I am not saying that you can't ever take off your makeup, or that you shouldn't wear comfortable shoes and clothing around your husband. If he is like my husband, he likes it when you are comfortable. Our goal isn't to look like Victoria's Secret models. God made all of our bodies different and each one of us is beautiful in His sight. There really is a balance to all of this. What I am saying can be boiled down to this: There really should be nights when you try not to look your absolute worst as you get into bed with your husband.

Consider a mother-in-law's point of view:
One of my greatest joys is to see how my son and daughter-in-law light up when they greet each other.

Be the daughter-in-law you hope to have:
- Avoid sleeping in while your husband leaves for work.
- Get some exercise.
- Cut one unhelpful thing from your life this week (soda, dessert, or fast food, for example).
- Touch up your makeup, and put on a clean shirt right before your husband walks through the door, or, if your kids are in bed, maybe no clothes at all (sorry, Mom)!
- Pray for the strength to discipline your body.

> *"Health and cheerfulness naturally beget each other."*
> —Joseph Addison

Love Him With Your Mind

Who can find a virtuous and capable wife? She is more precious than rubies. Her husband can trust her, and she will greatly enrich his life.
Proverbs 31:10-11 NLT

What does your mind have to do with your capability to love your husband well? A lot. A capacity for understanding is a gift. I'm not just talking about an ability to expand your vocabulary or learn the United States presidents in order (not that there is anything wrong with either of those endeavors; each is admirable). But I'm talking about becoming an intentional student of your husband.

Here's an axiom: The better you know someone, the better you can love him. My husband made this point in a sermon nearly ten years ago, and I still think of it often. It is a simple concept, but it's important. When we become a student of people, what we learn can help us love them better.

In Genesis 4:6, in the story of Cain and Abel, God says to Cain, "Why are you angry? Why is your face downcast?" God is reading Cain's face; He is noticing the expression of someone He loves. This is one of many examples in Scripture in which the godly trait of noticing the condition of people is mentioned. Jesus, time and again, took note of the countenance of the individuals He encountered.

> When we become a student of people, what we learn can help us love them better.

God gives us the capacity to engage in a ministry of "noticing." And if we are intentional about studying our husbands, we are using our minds to love them well. If your husband is anything like mine, he doesn't talk as much as you do, but he is communicating all the time. Sometimes we just need to ask questions to understand them better; sometimes we just need to understand them well enough to know questions are less than helpful. This is not an exercise in mental gymnastics or mind reading; it is relational intelligence that grows with time and effort.

Your mother-in-law probably will be able to assist you in this effort. She most likely will be thrilled to help. Again, she raised him, she knows him, and she loves him. If she knows you are asking questions about why he might be doing this or that, or what such and such means, so that you can love him better (not to tell on him, or get an upper hand), she can be a wellspring of helpful information. Take her out for a cup of coffee. Ask for her thoughts on what it means when your husband comes home from work and says, "I'm drowning. I am going for a run." He may have done the same thing in high school when he was under pressure or got a bad grade. Extra insight can't hurt because we all take certain traits with us as we age.

Knowing his history doesn't negate axiom number two: He's not the same man you married, and you aren't the same girl he married. This is pretty obvious, but change seems to take us by surprise no matter how constant it is. People change. That applies to your husband and you, and my husband and me. We can view change as a burden and sigh over the effort it takes to continue to learn about our husbands, or we can picture it as an extension of observations and conversations that caused us to fall in love in the first place. It's all a matter of perspective. When you were dating, discovering his interests and learning his desires was a part of the romance, a part of the fun. Why do we let that stop?

Love your husband well by being a lifelong learner, becoming conversant about things he cares about. That doesn't mean you have to study quantum mechanics if your husband is a physicist. It doesn't necessarily mean you have to learn about fishing if your husband loves to fish. He may not need you to share all his interests or one-up him in his areas of expertise, but you should know enough about some of his passions to understand why they excite him.

I don't know Greek or Hebrew, two languages my husband studies regularly, and I don't feel compelled to learn either language. However, when I do Bible studies, we talk about some of the nuances missed in the English translation of the Scriptures. To other people, that conversation might be boring, but he likes it, and I do, too.

What we think about, what we put into our minds, matters. And equally important in shaping our thoughts is what we keep out of it. With regard to the way you love your husband, sometimes what you keep out is more important. You don't need all the psychological research (and there is a lot out there) about the law of exposure to know what it is. The law of exposure is simply this: Your mind will think most about what it is most exposed to. Jesus puts it like this: We're storing up things in our hearts, our inner lives, all the time, good or bad, true or false, noble or demeaning (Luke 6:45).

In psychology, the law of exposure is almost always coupled with the law of cognition. The gist of that law: What enters our minds repeatedly occupies our minds, eventually shapes our minds, and, ultimately, will shape who we become. We can only offer others what we have available to share.

Therefore, we need to guard our minds against things that will hinder our ability to love our husbands well. Subtle things are the most dangerous. We have to watch out for the temptation to envy: "Why doesn't my husband buy me flowers like Betsy's husband buys for her?" "Why doesn't my husband say sweet things like Ryan Gosling does in The Notebook?" Comparisons like that not only are unhelpful, but they will kill contentment.

Paul offered the best solution for equipping our minds for God's purposes: "Whatever is true, whatever is honorable, whatever is right, whatever is pure, whatever is lovely, whatever is of good repute, if there is any excellence and if anything worthy of praise, dwell on these things" (Philippians 4:8, NASB).

Consider a mother-in-law's point of view:
My daughter-in-law is adorable, but she doesn't seem to have anything in common with my son anymore. She has her interests, and he has his. I'm going to pray that they will find some things that they enjoy talking with each other about or doing together.

Be the daughter-in-law you hope to have:
- Pay attention to your husband; study him.
- Do not be afraid to get helpful information about him from his mom.
- Ask your husband what the top three things are that he most enjoys. You can learn about them and learn from him. He won't mind.
- Be intentional about filtering what you let in and keep out of your mind. It matters.
- Pray for your thoughts to be pure.

> *"To a greater extent than we realize, and to a far greater extent than we would ever care to admit, we are what we read."*
> —STEVEN B. SAMPLE

Love Him With Your Soul

Just as lotions and fragrance give sensual delight,
a sweet friendship refreshes the soul.
PROVERBS 27:9

Pray and study Scripture. Let God's love flow through you.

The greatest thing you can do to love your husband well is to love Jesus. You will love your husband best if your soul is open to the love of Christ and your soul is opened through the love of Christ.

Each person who calls herself a Christian is on a spiritual journey with Christ. In his book *Sacred Pathways*, Gary Thomas reminds us to embrace our God-given temperaments and savor the uniqueness of our individual journeys. In other words, "Thou shalt not covet your neighbor's walk." Our journeys are most rewarding when we embrace spiritual disciplines. Praying, reading Scripture, and spending time in community with other Christians are means of grace that have served Christians well for centuries. They still work. We need to come to grips with the fact that there are no shortcuts.

We are called to be dependent on God first, and we cannot put our husbands or anyone else in God's place. It simply will not work. I don't care if you married Moses; no matter how great a man your husband is, he can't do God's work in your life. Without God's help, we fall short of being the women—and ultimately fail to be the wives—we could be with His help. God designed us to need Him. Once we commit to putting Him first, we are ready to make progress on sacred pathways of prayer, Bible study, worship, and Christian community. And because we are wives, our spiritual journeys overflow into blessings for our husbands and the overflow doesn't stop there. Our mothers-in-law are beneficiaries of those blessings as well.

A great way to pray well for your husband is outlined in Stormie Omartian's *The Power of a Praying Wife*. It has been around since 1997, but its message is timeless. I was skeptical at first, but it was helpful to me. It helped me know how specifically to pray for my husband and helped me to make a habit of bringing him before the Lord every day.

Next, study God's Word. Some study is primarily about finding out what Scripture has to say about God, but when in devotional study, the primary question switches from "What does this text say about God?" to "What might God be saying through this text to me?" Both questions are important. The first goes further in transforming your mind; the second goes further in filling your soul.

In addition to the disciplines of prayer and Bible study, you should find some friends who will encourage you, love you, and love Jesus. Ideally, your mother-in-law can be one of those friends. If she can't fit the bill, consider how much it would mean to you to be able to be that kind of Christian encourager to a future daughter-in-law. But for today, find some godly women who can pour into you.

If you can share any of these activities—praying, reading and discussing Scripture, or engaging in Christ-centered community—with your husband, count yourself blessed, and do it. It will only bring you closer as you strive to love your mother-in-law's son well.

Consider a mother-in-law's point of view:

I began to pray for my son's wife the day he was born. I hope my daughter-in-law will be encouraged by that and will consider praying for her son's future wife even now—not only for a woman who will make her son happy, but also for her to love Jesus and follow Him all the days of her life.

Be the daughter-in-law you hope to have:

- Take time to love and be loved by God.
- Pray daily for your husband.
- Read Scripture, and consider what God might be saying to you through His Word.
- Do life with people who love Jesus and love you . . . in that order.
- Pray for opportunities to bless your mother-in-law with the encouragements you are finding in your personal journey of faith.

> *"We are so grateful that we have a mother-in-law who prayed for us."*
> —Lisa, Lizzy, and Rhonda Hunter

Chapter Three

Just Be Kind

—Elizabeth Hunter

"**D**on't urge me to leave you or to turn back from you. Where you go I will go, and where you stay I will stay. Your people will be my people and your God my God. Where you die I will die, and there I will be buried. May the Lord deal with me, be it ever so severely, if anything but death separates you and me (Ruth 1:16-17 NIV)."

Can you imagine speaking these words to your mother-in-law? Ruth spoke these words to her mother-in-law, Naomi, after both women were widowed. An epitome of kindness to a mother-in-law is spoken in chapter 1 of the book of Ruth. We don't get a real sample of what their relationship was like before they both lost their husbands, but it is probably safe to assume that this was not one random act of kindness detached from the actual tone of their relationship. It is more likely that this is a culmination of many years of nurturing and growing their relationship.

Do Ruth's words indicate a relationship with her mother-in-law that is so far from the quality of your relationship with your mother-in-law that they cause you anxiety? Do you wince at the thought? How can we take steps toward being the type of daughter-in-law Naomi had? Admittedly, this was one grand gesture, but only striving toward excellence will distance us from mediocrity. Offering small gestures of kindness will definitely be a great starting point for bridging the disparity between your relationship with your mother-in-law and the luminary example of Ruth's relationship with hers.

Keep Intentions Pure

Since God chose you to be the holy people he loves, you must clothe yourselves with
tenderhearted mercy, kindness, humility, gentleness,
and patience. Make allowance for each other's faults,
and forgive anyone who offends you. Remember, the Lord forgave you,
so you must forgive others. Above all, clothe yourselves with love,
which binds us all together in perfect harmony.
Colossians 3:12-14 NLT

Intentions are motivators to action. An appropriate synonym for intention might be objective. When it comes to relationships, every action we choose is an effort to obtain a specific objective. Typical examples of this in my life can be found in many of my exchanges with my husband. When I say things like, "Ugh, I feel so fat today!" my intention is to gain reassurance that I am very thin. Too thin, in fact.

However, when I ask questions like, "Does my makeup make my face look orange?" or, "Do I look like I have a mustache?" my intention is to avoid public embarrassment. In these cases, compliments are counterproductive.

It is a delicate dance we dance.

Even our subconscious intentions can be our reaction motivators. If your mother-in-law has committed some offense, it might be difficult to show kindness to her. One's natural inclination, without necessarily thinking about it, might be passive aggression or even a passionate lashing out.

In order to give our best effort in a relationship with our mother-in-law, it is important that we examine our intentions before we act. If our intention is not relationship building, we may want to rethink our choice of action.

In some cases, a mother-in-law may feel unsettled about her daughter-in-law's intentions with her son. In this instance, a right step might be to make our intentions known. We may feel we have made our good intentions crystal clear through our actions, but we should never underestimate our mothers-in-law's insecurities. Our mothers-in-law may feel threatened. They may feel they are losing their sons. They simply may feel we don't like them. It won't hurt to clearly express to them that our intention is to make our relationships with them and the rest of the family a priority.

Not too long ago, I was talking with my friend Sara about her relationship with her mother-in-law. She told me that at one point, her mother-in-law had some fears, and those fears dominated her interactions with Sara. Sara's mother-in-law feared that her daughter-in-law didn't want to be a part of the family, and worried that her relationship with her son was slipping away.

What made the situation more difficult is Sara's mother-in-law never expressed her concerns openly to Sara. All news of these fears came to her "through the grapevine."

Sara had several choices of how to respond. She could react. She could allow herself to be insulted and decide to avoid her mother-in-law altogether—and, as a result, bring her mother-in-law's fears to fruition. This may have been the easiest response, but it also would have been the most destructive to the relationship.

Instead, Sara decided to broach the issue with her mother-in-law in a thoughtful, loving manner. She gave her a small gift, and when she presented it to her, she made clear her intentions. She expressed her concern that they had gotten off on the wrong foot and her desire to ameliorate their relationship. Her mother-in-law never acknowledged her fears; regardless, Sara was glad she had decided to reassure her mother-in-law that she was committed to being an involved member of the family alongside her husband.

Sara's intention in talking to her mother-in-law was not to corner her with, "I know what you've been saying." It was an effort to help her be comfortable in her role as a mother and, one day, grandmother.

So how do we know if our intentions are pure? Well, if our goal is to prove a point or teach a lesson, we will definitely want to reexamine our choice of actions. Generally, the lesson we try to teach is not the only lesson that is learned. Attempting to get even can only set us back. There are much better choices we can make to progress on the road toward a great relationship.

Consider a mother-in-law's point of view:
I wish I could read my daughter-in-law's mind. She probably would even tell me what I'd like to know if I asked her, but that doesn't seem like quite the right thing to do either. I really don't want to meddle in her life, but piecing together what her intentions are from the moments I do have with her can't be giving me a very accurate picture of how she thinks about things.

Be the daughter-in-law you would like to have:
- Be open with your mother-in-law. Express your intentions concerning your relationship with both her and her son.
- Avoid all temptation to get even with your mother-in-law, teach her a lesson, or prove your point. Any of these choices will result in hurt feelings.
- Pray and evaluate your intentions before choosing your action.

"Our actions are the results of our intentions and our intelligence."
—E. Stanley Jones

Pour Courage Into

*Speak encouraging words to one another. Build up hope
so you'll all be together in this, no one left out, no one left behind.
I know you're already doing this; just keep on doing it.*
1 Thessalonians 5:11

I happen to be blessed with a mother-in-law who is an incredible encourager. After a five-minute conversation with her, I walk away feeling like a superhero, which is befitting because to encourage means "to pour courage into."

I, on the other hand, am not a natural encourager. I am an excellent sharer, a great helper, but as an encourager, I fall short. I had never realized this shortcoming until I was married. My husband, who has his mother's knack for encouragement, started turning to her instead of me, his wife, for support and motivation. It was then I realized I needed to improve upon my courage-pouring skills. But before making strides toward improvement, I had to overcome being offended.

This was a good lesson for me to learn and one worth sharing: If your husband is turning to his mother on a regular basis, there may be a need of his that is not being met. It may sting at first to realize this, but instead of becoming insulted or even begrudging your mother-in-law for pulling your husband away from you, figure out how you can grow to better meet that need. Learn from your mother-in-law, and implement that lesson in your marriage. In this case, I needed to learn how to encourage better.

As I observed my husband and my mother-in-law, I realized what it meant to encourage. It was much more than a mere compliment. It was specific. It was enthusiastic. It was sincere. Sincerity—that is where I was struggling. I felt like once I spoke my one-liner, "I'm so proud of you," or, "You did great," saying any more would sound phony. In addition, it was uncomfortable for me. But I suppose strides toward improvement are rarely comfortable.

After many artificial-feeling attempts to encourage, it began to feel more natural. It even became comfortable. I've not yet arrived, but I'm much better and will continue to work toward being as encouraging as my mother-in-law, Becky Hunter.

Speaking of Becky Hunter, because she is such a great encourager, I never realized that she herself needed encouragement now and again. As foolish as it sounds, I saw how joyful and positive she was and subconsciously assumed she never felt discouraged.

Encouraging her will help minimize her insecurities. It wasn't until my mother-in-law took me on as her assistant when she was serving her term as president of the Global Pastors Wives Network that I realized I had really been subpar with my mother-in-law encouragement. As I worked closely with her, I got to see her come up against challenges in her very demanding position. One day as we were discussing the ministry, I said a measly, "You're doing great!" and she, to my surprise, responded by thanking me profusely for the praise. I couldn't believe I had been so negligent in that area! This woman needs to be encouraged just like every other person on the planet. I was in the perfect position to help pour courage into my mother-in-law and build our relationship, but I had been oblivious to it.

From that epiphany onward, I have made a deliberate effort to really encourage her. It is an important component to a solid relationship. Every living human has insecurities, and your mother-in-law's interaction with you may be a result of her own. Encouraging her will help minimize her insecurities. If you are struggling to find something positive, reflect upon the man you fell in love with. She raised that man. Try starting there, and see where it takes you.

Consider a mother-in-law's point of view:

I would love to get better at encouraging my daughter-in-law. Her responses to my kudos are hard for me to interpret. I can never tell if things I say or do to encourage her actually do that. But if what I say to her, and about her to others, encourages her even a fraction of how much she encourages me now and again, then I am certainly going to continue "pouring courage into" her the best ways I know how.

Be the daughter-in-law you would like to have:

- Practice encouraging your mother-in-law. Eventually, it will feel natural to "pour courage into" her.
- Try to be specific in your encouragement. It is more than just a compliment.
- Send notes or e-mails to encourage your mother-in-law.
- Tell her you love her.
- Pray for her, and let her know you are doing so.

> *"There is hardly any personal defect which an agreeable manner might not gradually reconcile one to."*
> —JANE AUSTEN

Be a Woman of Your Word

In the same way, their wives are to be women worthy of respect, not malicious talkers
but temperate and trustworthy in everything.
1 Timothy 3:11 NIV

I love to cook. I have a limited repertoire, but those dishes on the list are quite excellent. At least that is what my father always told me. But then, his favorite Thanksgiving treat is the main course's heart, so one may have reason to question his palate. (See chapter 1 for details.)

Being confident in my six to ten dishes, I didn't really value my husband's issues with some of their ingredients, mainly the bell peppers. I have a recipe for chili that I love to make, and my turkey heart-loving family seems to love my making it. In it, I put several chopped bell peppers.

After making the recipe a couple of times for my husband, he gently requested that I omit the bell peppers. What?! Chili without peppers is like beans without rice. Like coffee without cream. Like bacon without eggs. And although all of those things can stand on their own, making them inapplicable examples, his favorite food is hot dogs, so obviously he didn't understand my culinary prowess. He only thought he didn't like bell peppers.

But what if he didn't know that there were bell peppers in the dish? What if he couldn't see them? Then he would still like the chili, and I would be able to reveal to him that he did like bell peppers and that he just didn't like the way they looked. Now that I've typed it out, I do see some holes in my logic.

Nevertheless, I minced those red (because they camouflage themselves the most easily) bell peppers until they were almost a paste. It took a really long time, but it would all be worth it once I proved to Joel how much he liked bell peppers. I made the recipe as usual, but with a touch more hubris over how clever I was. When he ate the chili, he gave it high praise. He loved it. He loves bell peppers.

I waited a few days to reveal to him his newfound love for this food he didn't think he liked. He was going to be so pleased with me when I told him, "I told you so."

I gently reintroduced the topic of, "You think you don't like peppers," to which he naturally responded, "I don't like peppers."

"Aha! You loved the chili I made, and what you didn't know is that there were peppers in the chili. I had just chopped them so finely that you didn't know they were there, and you still liked it because you just think you don't like peppers, but you do. You love them."

"I'm so relieved that you brought that up. I didn't know if I should say anything about that. I even called my mom to ask her how I should deal with the situation because you kept putting peppers in my food and were even starting to chop them up really tiny so I wouldn't notice. She actually told me not to bring it up."

"You knew they were there?"

"Yes."

"Oh."

He then expressed to me how he didn't really like when I hid vegetables in his food like he was a toddler. I told him I was sorry and that I believed that he didn't like bell peppers after all.

He handled the situation graciously, but he also developed a distrust of me with recipe ingredients. As I would cook meals, he started to ask what I was putting in the dish. He began to make frequent trips through the kitchen to give my cutting board the once over. It eventually became a source of discord in our relationship.

"I know what I'm doing! Just let me cook," I would say.

"I'm just so worried you're going to put bell peppers in my food."

"I'm not. I don't understand why you hate my cooking!" Somehow to me that was the logical next point.

This was incredibly frustrating to me, but Joel felt he needed to implement his own system to ensure he was being considered in my culinary decisions. He had to trust in his own efforts because he couldn't trust me.

Intentionally or unintentionally, we sometimes make it difficult for people to feel they can rely on us. We may feel our mothers-in-law are forcing themselves into our lives when they are really only implementing a system to have themselves included because they don't feel they can trust that we will make the effort to include them. Try making plans with your mother-in-law in advance. And when those plans have been made, stick fast to them. Be reliable. A mother-in-law should not have to end up feeling she needs to grapple for a position in the family.

Prove to her that you are trustworthy. Keep your commitments. Be on time. Respond to e-mails and phone calls. Don't be afraid to apologize if you falter. Doing these things communicates to your mother-in-law that she is a priority, that her position is secure, that you love her.

As we work toward having a great relationship with our mothers-in-law, let's be women of our word. Let's not give it with a grain of salt. Relationships are built on a foundation of trust that we can choose to develop.

Consider a mother-in-law's point of view:

Sometimes I feel I have to force myself on my son's family, or I will never see them. Without her invitation, it's a bit tricky for me to discern whether my daughter-in-law is going to be expecting me to be somewhere or totally surprised if I show up. I depend on her more than she would assume I do for information about and invitations into their lives.

Be the daughter-in-law you would like to have:

- Initiate the making of plans. Make commitments with her, and keep them.
- If you are forgetful, make notes to yourself or set phone alarms so you do not miss an engagement with your mother-in-law.
- Return phone calls and e-mails. Don't give her a reason to fear that you may be distancing yourself.
- Be punctual, and call ahead if something prevents you from being on time.
- Pray that you will be trustworthy in your relationship with her, regardless of the trustworthiness of her interaction with you.

> *"A man's word and his intestinal fortitude are two of the most honorable virtues known to mankind."*
> —JIM NANTZ

Chapter Four

Address the Unreasonable

—Elizabeth Hunter

D YNAMICS BETWEEN A mother-in-law and her daughter-in-law are seldom pressure-free. Whether we have just recently entered into this new, foreign relationship, or we feel like veterans, having years' experience under our belts, there is no doubt that we feel the weight of expectations. Often we place this pressure on ourselves in an effort to prove that we are good wives and mothers. Other times we experience the pressure to live up to expectations that have been placed on us by our husbands' mothers. What do we do when such expectations overstep our boundaries?

Handle Expectations—Lovingly

Do not let any unwholesome talk come out of your mouths,
but only what is helpful for building others up according to their needs, that it may

benefit those who listen. And do not grieve the
Holy Spirit of God, with whom you were sealed for the day of redemption.
Get rid of all bitterness, rage and anger, brawling and slander,
along with every form of malice. Be kind and compassionate to one another,
forgiving each other, just as in Christ God forgave you.
EPHESIANS 4:29-32 NIV

Expectations are part of every relationship. We expect certain things from our loved ones, and they have certain expectations of us. As wives, we may feel a healthy pressure from mothers-in-law who expect us to love their sons well. They also may expect a certain kind of treatment from us. They may expect to be able to spend time with our families and us, or to be respected by their grandchildren. All of these are reasonable expectations. What do we do, though, when our mothers-in-law's expectations become unreasonable? How do we know when her presumptions have become presumptuous?

I was recently talking to my mother about her relationship with her mother-in-law. I had known that she and my abuelita (that's Spanish for "grandma"— not her first name, as I thought for the first ten years of my life) had their differences, but I never knew the full extent of the turmoil until recently. My Hispanic grandmother moved to New York City by way of the Dominican Republic. My mother, of Pennsylvania Dutch descent, grew up in a small town near Amish country. The two definitely had some cultural differences. Like water and oil. Like whoopie pies and frijoles negros. Like Shirleyann and Josefa Altagracia.

My abuelita had a habit of visiting my parents with little notice and even less discussion. She lived in close enough proximity to easily travel to their home, but not close enough to just stop in for a quick afternoon visit. She generally would announce her visit to my father and come with a packed bag, prepared to stay indefinitely.

After a few of these visits, my mother started to become frustrated with the situation. Finally, after the birth of their first child, my brother Daniel, the frustration came to a head. My abuelita came for a visit to spend time with the new grandbaby. After staying for a few days, it became apparent she hadn't set a date to leave. With more company coming into town, plus the stress of being a first-time parent, my mother's patience was running thin.

After asking my abuelita when she might leave and hearing her say she wanted to stay longer and spend time with the next batch of company, my mom blew a fuse. She demanded that my abuelita leave by telling her she was going to take her to the bus stop first thing the next morning. This did not go over well.

Harsh words were exchanged, and, as my father described, "It went from zero to ninety in a minute, with no chance for mediation." That would be slow for a car, but is quick for a fight. The result was both women crying and angry in respective corners of the apartment. My father went back and forth from wife to mother trying to smooth things over, with no success. Both were angry, hurt, and refusing to give any ground to the other. My father finally called their pastor to come help mediate. The mediation was unsuccessful. My mother refused to say she was sorry, and my abuelita said she was sorry—that my dad had married her.

The damage done to the relationship in this one explosive instance was devastating. It was many years before their relationship finally began to heal from that experience.

Although this is an extreme example, the theme of unreasonable expectation is a common one. My abuelita had an unreasonable expectation. She expected to be able to stay with my parents whenever she wanted for however long she wanted. I have read story after story of similar circumstances. Much like this example, the episode often occurs after the birth of a child. Unfortunately, in my mother's experience, things were handled in a way that was destructive to the relationship, rather than constructive.

The time period after the birth of a child is the absolute most difficult time to handle conflict well. Those postpartum hormones are no joke. The combination of hormones and conflict can result in some very passionate outbursts. If we foresee a tense situation, it might be best to discuss the issue ahead of time. When I had my son, I wasn't sure how well I was going to handle company, so I told my family that I would need to play the sleeping arrangements by ear, so they were prepared in case I didn't feel I could invite them into our home. In the case of a new baby, don't hesitate to have your husband address the situation with his mother. He probably will be more protective of you and the child than you realize. If enlisting him is unsuccessful or he can't seem to sway his mother's decision, you may have to do the dirty work yourself.

Before deciding to confront your mother-in-law, try to view the situation from her perspective. What you find unfathomable may seem completely reasonable to her. In my mother's situation, there was an extreme cultural barrier. In my abuelita's culture, it was completely reasonable for her to be welcomed into her son's home whenever she chose to visit. In my mother's culture, this supposition would be considered rude. You may be in a situation in which your mother-in-law views you as a child because you are her daughter-in-law, and imposing her will on you makes sense to her if she's the parent. Controlling your temper, being cool under fire and kind under duress, are all decidedly "grown-up" approaches to this type of conflict. Actively commanding the role of an adult in the conversation by these methods may be your responsibility if your mother-in-law isn't treating you like an adult.

Compromise doesn't make us weak; it makes us loving. It is never fun to confront another person about an issue, but it may be necessary in order to preserve a relationship. Remember that the reason for trying to improve the relationship is because you care enough about it to work on it. If you can't muster the courage to confront your mother-in-law in conversation, or you think your emotions might lead the conversation astray, consider other options. A well-thought-out letter or e-mail can work wonders. Invite your husband to edit it for you. He knows her well and will know the best way to communicate with her.

Before making the decision to address an issue with her, you may want to re-examine your position. Is standing your ground really your best option? You aren't a wimp just because you make some concessions now and then. Compromise doesn't make us weak; it makes us loving. Is there a compromise you can make? If not, is there a way you can agree to simply cooperate?

When addressing unreasonable expectations with your mother-in-law, it is key to do so lovingly. Even if she doesn't reciprocate with a loving response, leave the door open to mend the relationship.

Consider a mother-in-law's point of view:
If someone asks me, I can honestly say that if my daughter-in-law is a great wife to my son and a great mom to my grandchildren that is truly enough. Saying that is not difficult. Living like I mean it is.

Be the daughter-in-law you would like to have:
- Try to view the situation from your mother-in-law's perspective when dealing with unreasonable expectations. Is there a difference in culture? Is she trying to parent you?

- Write a letter or e-mail to express yourself to your mother-in-law if you are hesitant to speak with her about an issue.
- Choose a time when you are not heated to address issues you have with your mother-in-law. Regain your composure before trying to solve your problem.
- Pray and approach conversations with your mother-in-law as a loving, kind adult.

> *"Peace is not the absence of conflict; it is the ability*
> *to handle conflict by peaceful means."*
> —RONALD REAGAN

Control Moods

> *So, chosen by God for this new life of love, dress in the wardrobe*
> *God picked out for you: compassion, kindness, humility, quiet strength,*
> *and discipline. Be even-tempered, content with second place,*
> *quick to forgive an offense. Forgive as quickly and completely*
> *as the Master forgave you. And regardless of what else you put on,*
> *wear love. It's your basic, all-purpose garment. Never be without it.*
> COLOSSIANS 3:12-14

As members of the human race, we struggle with mood swings. Other than the annoyance of making us feel irrationally emotional, moods seem to take their toll mostly on others, as they affect how we treat them. Generally, those closest to us bear the brunt of the maltreatment.

I have always considered myself fairly unemotional. I was never much of a crier, although when I bragged about how little I cry to my husband, Joel, he said, "Really? Maybe you don't cry a lot for a girl." I don't cry a lot. He cries a lot.

I always attributed my stoicism to the fact that I grew up with three brothers. Crying was a source of ridicule between my brothers and me. As a result, I had an excellent gift of making it through sad movies without shedding a tear— that is, as long as a dog doesn't die in the end.

Unfortunately (for my husband), all my mettle seemed to melt away as soon as I became pregnant with our son. I started crying at every opportunity, at commercials and songs and even certain poignant episodes of "The Cosby Show." Olivia's birthday party episode is a real tearjerker. They grow up so fast.

Joel, as the supportive husband he is, would try to comfort me during my tearful episodes until it got to a point where I would just have to respond, "Please, ignore this. It's just what I do now." Thinking I would be rid of this emotional weakness once I had the baby, I was in for quite a shock when that time finally came. After the birth, my moods became more pronounced. Tiny things my husband would do or not do would send me into a weepy frenzy.

About a week after our son's birth, my husband had to go out of town for a conference. His mom, my mother-in-law, had just been in town and had kindly helped me get his clothes together for his trip. She even steamed them and gave us a tutorial on the best way to pack to avoid touch-ups. She really does have an impressive technique.

Still recovering from surgery, I wasn't mobile enough to pack my husband's clothes for him in the styling of Becky Hunter. Joel laid his suitcase on our living room floor and proceeded to pack his freshly pressed wardrobe under my close supervision. As I instructed him in the ways of his mother, he became frustrated with the scale of the project and just decided to pack how he normally does. The following conversation ensued:

Joel: I think I'm just going to pack how I normally do, and if I have to touch things up, I have to touch things up.
Me: (lip quivering) But your mom worked so hard to show us how to do it.
Joel: I know, but we don't really remember exactly how she did it, and this worked fine befo . . . .
Me: (weeping/yelling) YOU'RE JUST BEING SO CARELESS!
Joel: Okay, okay. I'm sorry. I'll pack the way she showed us.
Me: Sniffle. Thank . . . sniff . . . you.

In this instance, I chose to react according to my crazy, crazy mood. I didn't pause to think that Joel was packing his clothes, that he would have to iron them if they got wrinkled. I let my emotions direct my actions, and the result was my yelling unintelligibly at my husband. In the end, I did get what I wanted, but it wasn't very relationship-building.

It can become even more difficult to choose our reaction if the frustrating situation is recurring. We all have days when we don't get sleep or we are stressed or our husbands aren't packing right. Any small annoyance can act as a detonator. If your mother-in-law is consistently doing something that bothers you, it will be tempting to confront her when she does it when you are in a less patient mood. That will be the easiest time, but it also almost certainly will be the worst time. Wait until the dust on your frustration has settled; talk to her once the instance has passed. Pop (my father-in-law) once pointed out that emotions and reason can be thought of as sitting on opposite sides of a teeter-totter. When one side is high, the other will be at a low. Wait until reason is dominating to address important issues.

If discussing the issue with your mother-in-law doesn't seem to help, if she's unwilling to alter her behavior or the discussion escalates into an argument, this may be a good time to try to enlist your husband to help mediate. If he doesn't want to be involved, however, you can't force him. You can pray for a resolution and pray that he might want to be a part of that, but you cannot bend him to do your will. In fact, attempts to coerce him—calling him a "mama's boy" or trying to make him feel embarrassed in order to manipulate him into assisting in the process—are guaranteed to drive him further away from involvement and further away from you.

If you do decide to involve your husband in your differences with your mother-in-law, whether they are pivotal or petty, it is important to have a discussion based on concrete goals of resolution. Cornering him to complain about her will only make him shut you out. After all, the woman who has offended you is the woman who raised him, and a level of respect should be maintained. If nothing else, it is bad strategy to isolate him as the only one left to defend her.

In the same vein, try to refrain from ever speaking ill of your mother-in-law to your children. Grandparents are a blessing to children, and vice versa. I loved my grandmothers deeply, and although both of my parents had differences with their respective mother-in-law, they never shared it with us. They wanted our relationship with our grandmothers to be loving and healthy. Once you have tainted your child's perception of his or her grandmother, it is difficult to reverse it.

Moods are difficult to keep a rein on. For me, it can be a daily struggle. I am certain of this because as I was writing this chapter, I said to Joel, "Can you think of a specific example of a time I reacted to you because of a mood I was in?"

"Every time I've tried to talk to you in the morning."

"No. Not every time. Really?"

"Yeah. Our marriage took an upswing once we decided not to talk in the morning."

Clearly, I need to avoid falling victim to my own mood swings, specifically before 10 A.M. If you wait until the mood passes to discuss matters with your mother-in-law, you may be surprised at how positively she reacts. She may be just as eager as you are to better the relationship. If we make a habit of not reacting according to our moods, but pausing to control our actions, our relationships surely will "take an upswing."

Consider a mother-in-law's point of view:

I really appreciate when my daughter-in-law just comes to me if she has an issue with something I'm doing. When she is honest with me, I have the information I need to have a real chance to fix the problem and improve our relationship.

Be the daughter-in-law you would like to have:

- Try to avoid reacting in the moment to your mother-in-law's behavior. Wait until reason is above emotion on the "teeter-totter."
- Avoid beginning phrases with, "You always . . .," or, "You never . . ." when addressing an issue with your mother-in-law. Be sure to let her know you are coming to her because you love her and you don't want an issue, which you find troubling, to stand in the way of your relationship.
- Discuss your mother-in-law's actions with your husband when you are trying to strategize a resolution of differences. Be respectful of both him and his mother; don't use this time to whine or complain.
- Pray for that biblical kind of "peace that passes understanding," a steady temperament that keeps reason high on the "teeter-totter."

"Have the courage to act instead of react."
—OLIVER WENDELL HOLMES

Love Appropriately

*So this is my prayer: that your love will flourish and that you will not only
love much but well. Learn to love appropriately. You need to use your head
and test your feelings so that your love is sincere and intelligent,
not sentimental gush. Live a lover's life, circumspect and exemplary,
a life Jesus will be proud of: bountiful in fruits from the soul, making Jesus Christ
attractive to all, getting everyone involved in the glory and praise of God.*
PHILIPPIANS 1:9-11

We may be in a situation in which the relationship issues with our mothers-in-law go beyond the simple unexpected visits or insults to cookery capabilities. We may be facing a moral disagreement. This is a situation in which we feel our families are being negatively impacted by our mothers-in-law's life choices. Discernment in these circumstances is crucial. What can we do if we find ourselves in a tough spot, caught between helping them and protecting our families?

1. Judge without being judgmental.

It is completely natural, not to mention healthy, to want to protect our families. Our husbands' and children's well-being should always be our priority. If you view your mother-in-law's lifestyle choices as a threat to your family, before you take any course of action, you need to objectively decide whether what she is doing is, in fact, a detriment, or just not your personal preference.

What is it about your mother-in-law's lifestyle that troubles you? Is it something she does outside of her interaction with you and your family? She may go to bars. She may have an affinity for casino cruise ships. She may have forty-five cats. You may not like how she invests her time and money, but is it directly affecting her interaction with you, your husband, and your children? Let's try to avoid writing off a mother-in-law as a "bad influence" simply because we disagree with her decisions or dislike how she spends her free time. Loving, nurturing mothers and grandmothers don't always look or act the ways we imagined or hoped they would. That alone doesn't mean they are less deserving of time with our, their, families.

On the other hand, your mother-in-law may swear like a sailor in front of your children. In a particularly volatile relationship, she may speak ill of you to them. These definitely would be good reasons to discuss appropriate behavior with her. We have the right and an obligation to filter the influences we allow into our children's lives. That isn't self-centeredness. It is good parenting. Once you have put the guidelines out there, she may well choose to censor herself, rather than miss out on time with her grandchildren. If she chooses not to honor your rules concerning your children, it is very reasonable to limit her interaction with them.

If your mother-in-law has issues with roots that go much deeper than simply not abiding by your rules, if she's dealing with substance abuse or another potentially devastating problem, that's a much more complicated situation. Of course, you are concerned for her, but if your children are getting exposed to things that aren't healthy for them to be around, you may, after seeking counsel from your husband and doing what you can to help her return to a healthy lifestyle, need to cut off personal interaction for however long it takes. Our children should not have to deal with more than is appropriate for their maturity level.

This point is well made in a story Corrie ten Boom wrote in her journal. At the age of ten, she was traveling on a train with her father, and she asked him to explain a word she had heard. It was a word that no little child should have to hear. Her father looked at her, as he always did when answering her questions, but said nothing. At last, he stood up, lifted his traveling case from the rack over their heads, and set it on the floor. "Will you carry it off the train, Corrie?" he asked. "It's too heavy," she said. "Yes," he said. "And it would be a pretty poor father who would ask his little girl to carry such a load. It's the same way, Corrie, with knowledge. Some knowledge is too heavy for children. When you are older and stronger, you can bear it. For now, you must trust me to carry it for you." She was satisfied and at peace with that answer. There are some things that children cannot and should not yet have to handle. And someday they will be glad you waited to share such heaviness until they could handle it with you.

2. Forget about "fixing."

In a circumstance in which a family member has an addiction, it is really tempting to try to fix that person. While we may need to cut off all interaction, and hope that action might make them want to change, ultimatums don't have a reputation for inspiring people to reinvent the way they live. The truth is, no one will get fixed unless he or she wants to get fixed. Our responsibility is to pray for and love them. As Pop, my husband's father, says, "You can't fix them. You can only love them."

3. Learn how to love.

In a situation in which your mother-in-law is living a questionable lifestyle, you must decide the best way to show your love for her. Our top priority should always be to show Christ's love and try to bring others closer to Him. All decisions should be run through this filter. If your case is extreme and you've had to separate her from your family, try to think of ways you can still let her know that you love her. Maybe you and your husband can pay her visits without the children. Be intentional about writing e-mails and calling regularly. Have your children write to her or draw pictures for her. And most importantly, pray for her.

It's so important to love actively in a situation like this. It is easy to become frustrated with someone who doesn't want to change. It may seem so easy for her to fix herself, but for her, it isn't easy. And while it is tempting to become hopeless under these circumstances, our job is to pray for her and love her. Whether she takes steps toward change or not, love her because Christ loves her.

Consider a mother-in-law's point of view:

Somehow my son turned out just fine. Even my daughter-in-law must think so; after all, she did marry him. But I can't seem to convince her that I am capable of caring for my grandchildren. Maybe she is just a natural worrier, but if it's more than that, I need to know her specific concerns.

Be the daughter-in-law you would like to have:

- Use objective discernment to decide whether your mother-in-law's lifestyle is negatively affecting your family, or is just subjectively offensive to you.
- Care for and protect your family. That is your priority, and it is completely acceptable to separate your family members from anything that would jeopardize their well-being.
- Address situations with your mother-in-law through a loving filter.
- Pray and treat her lovingly. Don't give up on your mother-in-law.

> *"He has a right to criticize, who has a heart to help."*
> —ABRAHAM LINCOLN

Chapter Five

Add Insight

—Lisa Hunter

"INSIGHT INTO HUMAN NATURE ... what compulsions drive a man, what instincts dominate his action ... if you know these things about a man you can touch him at the core of his being" - William Bernbach.

A little insight, a little understanding can go a long way in helping us love someone well. Bernbach's comment made more specific to our relationships with our mothers-in-law would read, "Insight into human nature . . . what compulsions drive your mother-in-law, what instincts dominate her action . . . if you know these things about your mother-in-law, you can touch her at the core of her being."

The hope for this book is for you to have a healthy, happy relationship with your mother-in-law, and that is more likely if you understand her, appreciate her, and love her for who God made her to be. The better we understand how people act in general, the better equipped we are to understand our mothers-in-law and the more able we are to build healthy relationships with them. I love the way my husband, Josh, describes the power of insight:

"Good insight comes with being able to 'put yourself in another person's shoes'—being able to see things from his or her perspective. When you can do that, you gain wisdom about how the person feels, and, as a result, you are better able to communicate with that person in ways he or she will understand."

When you know what makes your mother-in-law tick and why she reacts a certain way, your relationship can be so much better, and conversations are likely to be much smoother.

Insight into the way she deals with issues of faith, times of transition, and concerns about the future will be especially helpful to you as you try to love your mother-in-law well. Learn what "makes her tick" and why she reacts a certain way. Pay attention to these areas of her life. These are insights that can help you do your part!

Put God First

Those who seek the Lord lack no good thing.
PSALM 34:10B NIV

Faith in Jesus Christ is the Cornerstone for insight. That insight encourages us to join our lives with His and bring His love, compassion and, hopefully, His perspective into all of our relationships. Our best possible connections with our mothers-in-law can be seen through the insight that Jesus gives us. Through Him, we can look past the things we do not agree with, past the different methodologies they use, and beyond personalities that are nothing like our own. Our faith will let us love our mothers-in-law with a Christlike love, even if we are struggling to "put ourselves in their shoes" and see things from their points of view.

If you and your mother-in-law are Christians, you have common ground! Your shared faith in Christ and desire to do what He asks of you is a great place to start building your relationship. In fact, there is no better place! That doesn't mean it won't require any work; relationships are very complex. Sometimes, I think God must have a sense of humor, giving me some of the relationships that He has given me. How is it that the very thing He made us for (relationships) is one of the most difficult things? I truly think it is because as we learn how to build meaningful relationships, it helps us understand how to interact better with Him.

I am so blessed to have a mother-in-law who loves Jesus and knows Him very well, but my heart grieves for some of you reading this because your situation is different. Maybe your mother-in-law doesn't know Jesus. I can't begin to imagine what that's like for you, but let me encourage you by reminding you that your being in her life is not an accident. God is sovereign, and when you married your husband, everything that was part of him became part of you.

Insight has the power to change the trajectory of a relationship.

Keep doing everything you can to love her and be like Jesus to her, whether or not she shares your faith. In the immortal words of the band, Journey, "Don't Stop Believin'"! You never know what seeds are being planted by your faithfulness in loving her well.

When it comes to faith, believing in Jesus is more than just head knowledge. It means trusting Him, spending time with Him daily, having a relationship with Him. We can't really know or truly love someone unless we spend time getting to know him or her. The same is true with God. To love well the God who loves us takes dedicated time and effort.

We learn in Romans 8:29 that God "decided from the outset to shape the lives of those who love him along the same lines as the life of his Son." In other words, we are transformed through our understanding of Christ, and because of that transformation, we can see our mothers-in-law through new eyes. We can see them more like He sees them. And like He does, we will want the best for them and will encourage the best in them. So, with His insight, because we want the best for our mothers-in-law, we might agree to disagree, accept their ways of doing things, and learn to enjoy differences in our personalities. There is, however, also the possibility that a few of us might realize that our mothers-in-law are women who at their very core are far away from God, miserable, and lost. The only thing that we can do to encourage the best in them is to pray for them. God can give you the insight to see her as she should be instead of how she is in the moment.

That sure is helpful in situations in which you think your mother-in-law is totally insane! A godly perspective allows you to see why this is happening instead of focusing on what she is doing.

On the flip side, I've been very grateful during temporary moments of insanity when my mother-in-law has done just that! She could have handled it much differently, but because she has loved Jesus for years and because of her daily choice to live out her faith, she had the ability to be extremely compassionate, nonjudgmental, and, most of all, loving. Oliver Wendell Holmes said, "A moment's insight is sometimes worth a life's experience." When I think of the insight God gave her in those moments, I am so grateful. Insight has the power to change the trajectory of a relationship. When God is put first, everything else falls into place—so simple to say, so interesting to consider, so hard to do.

Consider a mother-in-law's point of view:
I love Jesus, and she loves Jesus, but the minute we go into any more detail than that, things get complicated.

Be the daughter-in-law you hope to have:
- Spend time with God every day. See His heart and get to know His character.
- Ask God to give you insight about your mother-in-law.
- Give your mother-in-law the benefit of the doubt. Choose to focus on the good in her.
- Spend time with her, and make an effort to get to know her better.
- Hear her out, and look for the why instead of focusing on what she's doing in the moment.
- Pray for her, and look for the ways God is working through her.

"We often think of great faith as something that happens spontaneously so that we can be used for a miracle or healing. However, the greatest faith of all, and the most effective, is to live day-by-day trusting Him. It is trusting Him so much that we look at every problem as an opportunity to see His work in our life."
—RICK JOYNER

Show Kindness During Transitions

And we know that in all things God works for the good of those who love him, who have been called according to his purpose.
ROMANS 8:28 NIV

With life, change is inevitable. The first day of school, marriage, the birth of a baby, a new job, relocation, and the death of a loved one are examples of change. Whether the transition is good or bad, easy to adapt to or agonizing, it will shape parts of our character for a long time to come.

There are so many examples of life's transitions we could talk about, and maybe this comes to mind just because the mother-in-law/daughter-in-law relationship is our topic, but I can't think of a better example of a person who feared change more than the lead character in the movie Monster-in-Law. Viola Fields (played by Jane Fonda) desperately and irrationally tried everything in her power to prevent change.

Here's the plot: Charlotte "Charlie" Cantilini (played by Jennifer Lopez), after many years of searching, finds the man of her dreams, Kevin Fields (played by Michael Vartan). When their relationship becomes serious and it's time to meet his mother, she finds his mom to be a nightmare. Viola is a recently fired prime time news anchor who is afraid she will lose her son the way she lost her career. Viola determines to scare off her son's fiancée by becoming the world's worst mother-in-law. Viola and her longtime assistant do their best to pull off some crazy plans. Charlie decides to fight back and she and Viola battle it out.

If you haven't seen it, and reading this plot causes you to imagine what some of the crazy schemes were, think worse! Actually, it really was a funny movie. I don't want to spoil it for those who haven't seen it, so I won't give away the ending, but the movie gives insight into what a mother-in-law/daughter-in-law relationship should not be. And it shows just what a person will sink to when insecurity and fear take over in order to get noticed, be loved, and feel needed.

As comedic as the movie is, the sad truth remains: Many mother-in-law/daughter-in-law relationships are that strained. Much of the time, it is because one or both parties are dealing with insecurity. When that is the case, any life transitions that come along, good or bad, magnify the nasty behaviors that come from being insecure—a sense of entitlement, instability, fear, jealousy, and so on. Take Viola's case. Instead of looking at the marriage of her precious son, Kevin, and future daughter-in-law, Charlie, as something to celebrate, she feared that she might not be needed anymore. She dreaded the thought of being replaced as the number one woman in her son's life. Ironically, her insecurity caused her to do the very things she hated doing and to become someone she despised; she "became" her own mother-in-law, Gertrude.

How can you and I as daughters-in-law act differently than Charlie and be able to gain insight into loving our mothers-in-law through life's transitions? I think one of the most important ways to do this is to put ourselves in their shoes.

If you can identify and relate to the reason for her behavior, "why she's acting like this," you will be able to see her in a different light. Don't forget that having a son marry was a huge transition for her. She wants to know that she still matters. Filling voids is God's job not ours, but we all are called to do our part in our relationships. Our part is to become a better person—a better listener, more compassionate, more generous, and those of us who are Christians should have evidence of the Holy Spirit in our lives. His presence in us makes us more loving, joyful, peaceful, patient, kind, good, faithful, gentle and self-controlled. Our part is never to try to change the other person in that relationship. Love her for who she is, and learn to appreciate where she is in her journey, and you may never have to face a monster-in-law.

Consider a mother-in-law's point of view:

My son fell in love, and I'm happy he has found someone to share life with, but I'm worried that his wife, might not help enough, care enough, encourage enough, work enough, play enough, or laugh enough. I'm afraid she might cry too much, play too much, work too much, spend too much, or complain too much. Hmm. Maybe I need to let this go.

Be the daughter-in-law you hope to have:
• Make no assumptions about your mother-in-law. Observe, listen, and ask questions, and before long, you will know her well.
• Ask her for advice, and give her the opportunity to speak into your life when it is appropriate to do so.
• Be slow to speak and quick to listen.

- Look for ways God is using your mother-in-law to bless others. Give her credit for her efforts.
- Pray that you will not wittingly or unwittingly give her reasons to react poorly toward you.

> *"If nothing ever changed, there'd be no butterflies."*
> —ANONYMOUS

Build Your Life With the Future in Mind

> *"For I know the plans I have for you," declares the Lord, "plans to prosper you and not to harm you, plans to give you hope and a future."*
> JEREMIAH 29:11 NIV

What you do today will shape your relationship with your mother-in-law in the future. Let's go back to the movie, Monster-in-Law and see how the rest unfolds. Near its end (don't worry this isn't a spoiler alert), Viola and her assistant have a heart-to-heart conversation, in which Viola comes unglued.

Viola: I cannot believe she compared me to Gertrude. (Viola's mother-in-law)
Assistant: I know. Now that's just wrong.
Viola: Thank you.
Assistant: You are far worse. I don't recall Gertrude ever trying to poison you. And I'm pretty sure she wore black to your wedding.
Viola: Black. Yeah, she said she was in mourning. I just want my son to be happy.
Assistant: Whatever made you think he wasn't?[1]

After the assistant says her last line in that conversation, pointing out that perhaps Viola's son is indeed happy, soft music starts, she walks out of the room, and the camera cuts to Viola. And we see a new side of her. She doesn't say a word, but her countenance drops. In that moment, her remorse is obvious, and we see a woman who desperately wishes it could all be taken back. Full of regret, sensing no possible relationship with her daughter-in-law in the future because of its current broken state, Viola was defeated.

I will let you watch the movie to find out what happens in the end, but here is what I will share with you: If you have a mother-in-law like Viola, someone with monster-like tendencies, give her grace. Your mother-in-law is important. A daughter-in-law who acts like Charlie, desperate and focused only on the present moment, has failed to see how her current actions can greatly damage their relationship in the future. Issuing paybacks, insisting always that we are right, and demanding to be heard are signs we have lost perspective.

How will I want my daughter-in-law to treat me?

Keeping perspective is key. Choosing not to engage in malicious or juvenile behavior with your mother-in-law will work to your benefit. If you haven't already established a good foundation for the relationship you hope to have with her in the future, then start now. As you learn things about her, the good and the bad, as you start to figure out what makes her tick, -- these are insights into her life. Knowing them now will benefit your relationship later.

God will use what you learn about your mother-in-law to increase your compassion and patience with her, and as you love her well, you will be more like Him.

There is one more reason why it is helpful to gain such insight with the future in mind. There's a good chance we will be mothers-in-law ourselves someday. We will be on the other side, so it is important for us to ask ourselves, "How will I want my daughter-in-law to treat me? Am I behaving toward my mother-in-law the way I would want my daughter-in-law to behave toward me?" Those questions to your "future self" will help you love your mother-in-law well, now.

Consider a mother-in-law's point of view:

When I was a girl, I thought about the future a lot. I wanted to be ten when I was eight and sixteen when I was twelve. I wanted to get a driver's license, get married, and have kids, and later I thought about getting to play with my grandchildren. There is always a future to aim for, and the days I remember that are more fun.

Be the daughter-in-law you hope to have:
- Find something about her that is positive. Confirm it by telling her.
- Find a negative feeling you have toward her, and let it go!
- Treat your mother-in-law the way you hope your daughter-in-law will treat you one day.
- Pray that you bring your mother-in-law joy.

"The future is always beginning now."
—MARK STRAND

Chapter Six

Prioritize Love and Patience

—Rhonda Hunter

I HAVE ALWAYS BEEN intrigued by people's behaviors and the choices they make. I chose to pursue a psychology degree in college not because listening to people's problems was something I enjoyed even though I try to be as empathetic as possible. I was fascinated by people's behaviors, and I loved collecting data for research. It was often the unexpected results of the studies that I found so intriguing.

In Psych 101, they teach you that even the tiniest variations in a control group will drastically change the outcome of your research.

I mention this because I realize none of us have the exact same "control" group. All of our stories with our mothers-in-law are different. We each have unique variables to deal with that make prioritizing love and patience in our relationships with our mothers-in-law a unique challenge. But, and this is the good news, we have the ability to change the results—by altering what we control. Just a few right choices in the right direction can drastically alter the trajectory of our relationships—and recognizing that may make all the difference.

Let's look at three variables we can control.

Wait for Proper Timing

Like apples of gold in settings of silver
is a word spoken in right circumstances.
PROVERBS 25:11 NASB

Imagine your mother-in-law comes into the delivery room right before you have your first child. You are pretty focused on the upcoming event, but trying to be kind. And so is she. But, she says, "Thank you so much for letting me be in here for a while—just so you know though, your sister-in-law is outside and she is pretty mad that she can't come in right now. But don't you worry about that—you should just be excited for this moment. You will probably be able to patch things up with her later."

Let's give her the benefit of the doubt, and assume her statement was made in an effort to be kind. But was it helpful? No. Why not? Bad timing. And even all the right words spoken at wrong times won't sound as they ought. The same words or actions can be medicine or poison, depending on the timing of delivery.

So what makes for good timing, or "right circumstances," in our relationships with our mothers-in-law? Two things: first, our own state of mind in delivering help or offering "wisdom," and second, careful consideration of our mothers-in-law's conditions, stress levels, and capacity to hear what's being said or to rightly interpret what's being done.

An often overlooked element of knowing whether it's the right time to say something is how you are feeling when you say it. The proper timing of kind and complimentary words is generally easy. As long as you are not shouting over other people, you can pretty much say whatever kind things you please, as you please.

However, the timing of more difficult conversations requires further thought and self-awareness. For example, if your mother-in-law has just told you she is going to "go out and do some exercise on your behalf, since you can't seem to get out there and do it yourself," an immediate reaction likely will not be as helpful in the long run as a delayed planned response.

If you are frazzled and tired and ready to cry for one reason or another at the end of a Thanksgiving extravaganza, and your mother-in-law reprimands your child in a way that you wish she wouldn't, it is probably wise to wait a little while till the time is better for both of you to address it. This delay will help you say what you really think needs to be said, instead of saying what you feel like saying in the moment.

If you are too angry in a moment to love a person well, you are likely also too angry to love the person wisely, which means to have right words spoken into the "right circumstance," you will have to wait.

Of course, it's not just your own state of mind that influences right timing. Your mother-in-law's thoughts and feelings are an integral part of the timing equation. If you do not take them into consideration, your solutions will be wrong. For example, if she is trying to get a family picture organized and you tell her just before the picture is snapped, "You might want to find someone new to do your hair because the past couple of cuts have left you looking much older than you actually are," that's bad timing. Even if you could figure out a nicer way to say that, and give her the salon information she would require to resolve her hair issues, it's still the wrong time.

More often than not, good timing requires just a little bit of insight, sensitivity, and patience on the part of the communicator. It is a small thing that makes a big difference over the long haul.

Consider a mother-in-law's point of view:
I need to remember that my timing is not perfect, and I should not expect that my daughter-in-law's would be either.

Be the daughter-in-law you would like to have:
- Ask yourself before you comment on something, "Is this the right time to say this?"
- Take note of the setting and circumstance. Consider your mother-in-law's feelings before you make a point or take action.
- Pray before you engage her in a conversation that could be difficult, and schedule a time to have it.

"The only reason for time is so that everything doesn't happen at once."
—Albert Einstein

Demonstrate Flexibility and Kindness

A soldier on duty doesn't get caught up in making deals
at the marketplace. He concentrates on carrying out orders. . . .
Think it over. God will make it all plain.
2 TIMOTHY 2:4, 7

Easygoing, accommodating, cooperative . . . we love these kinds of people. These are the kinds of people we want around us—the kinds of girlfriends who laugh instead of scoff when we make mistakes, who offer grace instead of judgment when we err. They make life simple and, if the truth be told, more fun. It's a given that if we had the choice, we would surround ourselves with kind and flexible people, rather than unkind, inflexible ones. But the question to ask ourselves is, "What kind of people will we choose to be?"

If your mother-in-law heard you answer that question, would she agree with the way you see yourself? Does she see you as flexible and accommodating, or demanding and stubborn? Would she describe you the same way always, or can something like a special event—a holiday, birthday, or vacation—cause her to revise her description?

Though it is difficult to be flexible and accommodating, we love it when other people are. We can understand why they are great to be around. But those attributes are difficult for most of us to embrace and apply in familial relationships. And they may be particularly difficult in our relationships with our mothers-in-law for one very simple reason: We like to be in control. And chances are pretty good that she does, too.

However, there are times when we should willingly surrender our control of events and details, and yield the picture in our minds of the way we think things ought to be for the sake of relational harmony.

True kindness is a result of God's work in our lives (Galatians 5:22). The Bible implies that kindness is a combination of sympathy and understanding, of benevolence and gentleness. In other words, it is impossible to demonstrate kindness without putting the needs of others above our own.

Being flexible enough with our own agendas to include our mothers-in-law's agendas does not mean we do everything they say or resign from the responsibilities God has given us as wives and mothers. We are adults, and we need to decide where to set the boundaries and where to build the bridges for our families. Communicate clearly, and do it sooner rather than later. That being said, there are far fewer instances than we might assume that warrant our insisting on our own way. If we choose to be easygoing, accommodating, and cooperative in our interactions with our mothers-in-law—remembering that we are not their Holy Spirit—they should feel no need to defend themselves or control us. They might actually relax and be comfortable around us.

Consider a mother-in-law's point of view:
I hate to be annoying, but I'm a mother-in-law so I have to be intentional about not being annoying or I will be. The more respectful I am of my daughter-in-law's perspective the more likely I am to bring joy rather than frustration to her, my son and their children.

Be the daughter-in-law you would like to have:
- Recognize that your mother-in-law might not be trying to make your life difficult by chasing you down for an answer to confirm a date, time, or place. She has to try to balance all other family members' schedules as she is planning an event.
- Do not make your routine the most important. Make yours the most flexible.
- Figure out what boundaries, if any, you and your husband must set. Be clear about what those are, and then be as flexible as you possibly can with the rest.
- Pray for the grace to be accommodating and adaptable even, and maybe especially, if your mother-in-law is not.

> *"Everybody thinks of changing humanity,*
> *and nobody thinks of changing himself."*
> —LEO TOLSTOY

Treasure Her

And mark that you do this with humility and discipline—not in fits and starts,
but steadily, pouring yourselves out for each other in acts of love,
alert at noticing differences and quick at mending fences.
EPHESIANS 4:3

Family members are often the hardest individuals to love, but Jesus didn't exclude them from the greatest commandment to "love one another." When we treasure people, we love them. "Where your treasure is, there your heart will be also." Matthew 6:21 NASB

You can value them in any number of ways. You treasure your mother-in-law when you invest time and energy in your relationship with her. You treasure her when you honor her, speak well of her to others, or send a card or gift to her now and then. You treasure her as you value the good she has accomplished and assume the best of her. You also treasure her when you treat her as she would like to be treated and do not just assume that what you consider to be a treat would be a treat for her as well. If you have no idea how to figure out what her likes and dislikes really are, and you have not read *The 5 Love Languages*, by Gary Chapman, reading that book could help you solve that mystery.

Do not just assume that what you consider to be a treat would be a treat for her as well.

In that book Chapman talks about five effective ways we can express our heartfelt love for another person. He proposes that words of affirmation, quality time, gifts, acts of service and physical touch are among our best options for letting others know we love them. Now, we might assume that the expression of love we would most appreciate receiving is the one that our mother-in-law would most appreciate, as well. That could be the case, but it's highly unlikely.

To me, a day at a good spa is heaven. I like all of it—the massage, the free robes, all of it. However, that is not something that my mother-in-law enjoys. She will indulge in having her hair done or getting a manicure, but a spa is just not her thing. I could convince myself that if I took her to the "right" spa (and she participated in all the pampering), she would love it. I am sure she would appreciate my thoughtfulness but I know her, and she would much rather just have me tell her I really appreciate her than spend a day having, as she puts it, someone treat her "like a lump of dough." We don't find our differing opinions about such things annoying, in fact, they make us laugh.

How can you let your mother-in-law know that you treasure her? What are some things she enjoys, and how can you communicate your love for her through those things?

My son's teacher, Pam Massengale, told me a creative way she honors her mother-in-law. She got all of her mother-in-law's great recipes and whenever she bakes for any special occasion, she uses those recipes. Pam uniquely honors her mother-in-law by telling everyone who commends the delicious results that they should thank her mother-in-law because the recipe was hers.

Here's the bottom line. Find out what makes your mother-in-law feel loved and appreciated and then, when you do invest your time, energy, and talents in your relationship with her, she just might really believe you truly care about her.

Consider a mother-in-law's point of view:
I so appreciate my daughter-in-law's thoughtfulness toward me. As our family expands through each generation, I sometimes worry that my resources to bless each one are spread so thin that she and the others may not realize how much I treasure each one of them.

Be the daughter-in-law you would like to have:
• Educate yourself about some of the things your mother-in-law values so you are better able to appreciate them with her.
• Treasure her uniquely through your talents and time.
• Pray that she will be able to sense that you do treasure her.

"Next to excellence is the appreciation of it."
—WILLIAM MAKEPEACE THACKERAY

Chapter Seven

Value Her Son

—Lisa Hunter

W E DON'T CHOOSE our mothers-in-law; we just get them when we marry their sons. Some of us feel we "hit the jackpot" and get to be related to one of the most incredible people on the planet. Others of us, not so much. One thing that mothers-in-law seem to have in common with one another is their concern for the health and well-being of our marriages. And that makes sense. If you saw your son and his wife struggling in their marriage relationship, wouldn't that be a concern for you? If our relationships with our husbands are challenging, if we are not acting as one and focusing on our part in the marriage, it will affect those who are closest to us. No marriage is isolated. Those vows we made to each other meant something to our families as well.

Every marriage is unique. My story may not be at all similar to yours, but every story has the potential to save someone some heartache and offer encouragement. Here is a quick synopsis of my marriage. When we were first married everything was blissful, selfless, and wonderful. But soon after our first child was born, bliss turned into misery. Selflessness turned into selfishness and everything was not wonderful. Josh and I went through a couple of years that were very rough; they affected not only us, but also everyone we cared about. We got to the point where we didn't want to be in the same room together.

We were married, but living as singles. It was a two-year-long roller coaster of counseling, but we didn't give up. God was faithful and totally redeemed a marriage. Since 2001, our marriage has been a testimony to the fact that God still performs miracles. What He brought us through is a testimony of His grace, love, and forgiveness. I don't claim to be an expert on marriage, but I learned some tough lessons the hard way. And not to share with you what God has done in my marriage, and can do in yours, would be a disservice to Him.

During the time we were struggling, my mother-in-law was one of the people affected by our relationship. But through it all, she loved me every bit as much as she loved Josh. And she made sure I knew it. She did her best to give us space to work things out and prayed constantly for us. I know she wasn't the only person doing that, but I am grateful she was one of them. I feel close to her, because of the way she supported me during that difficult season.

Since coming out of that pit in 2001, I've had the opportunity to have lots of conversations with other wives. Many of them have issues with their mothers-in-law, but when we get down to the heart of the problem, the majority of the time, those issues stem from issues they have with their husbands. Their difficulties with their mothers-in-law are often a direct result of weaknesses in their marriages.

When we get married, we come into the relationships with expectations of who our spouses should be. Whether these expectations are realistic or ideal, they can become the very things that can drive us apart instead of together.

Have you ever said to your husband, "My dad never acted like that!" or, "If I say it again, maybe you will finally get it," or, "Why should I have to tell you? You should know how I'm feeling"? I know I have.

When I remember I have said things like that, it doesn't make me feel very proud, but those times are a good reminder to me not to say them again. God wants us to focus on doing our part in the relationship. Our job is to make sure we are doing what we can to help our husbands—not to take inventory or worry about what they should be doing for us. If we focus on our unmet expectations, life will not be how God intended it to be.

We are going to look at three perspectives wives can easily avoid.

You Are Not Your Husband's Mother

The Lord God said, "It is not good for the man to be alone.
I will make a helper suitable for him."
GENESIS 2:18 NIV

Women tend to be nurturers. It's amazing how this can be seen at a very young age when little girls play with their baby dolls or pretend to play house. They love to care for their babies or members of their pretend family, and often will create scenarios where they are needed. The baby doll got a cold and needs to take medicine, or her kids won't listen, so she does whatever is needed for them to, or the baby doll just simply won't stop crying until the little mommy holds her tight in her arms.

No matter our age, everyone has the need to feel needed. When we marry, we become wives who need to be needed. This need looks different in each marriage—personalities and temperaments vary—but the innate need to nurture will always be there.

In the garden, Eve felt the need to help because she was created as a partner for Adam. And we were, too, for our husbands. Because of this, there will always be a God-given desire to care for and help our husbands.

Men tend to be conquerors. This can be seen at an early age when a proud little boy crushes the Green Goblin with his amazing Web skills, or when boys (or men) wrestle like bear cubs to determine the king of the mountain. Men want to be in control and not be told what to do. Most value a very clear authority structure, and when someone outside of that authority attempts to fill a role that was not assigned, they become threatened or defensive. You may have heard arguing siblings or frustrated kids on a playground, or, heaven forbid, even your own husband declare, "You're not my mom!"

No matter the age, there is an understanding of authority, and a wife is not supposed to act like her husband's mom.

That is a big temptation for us, though, isn't it? So where do you think we miss the mark? Why is it that we feel if we are going to help our husbands, we must treat them like our kids? Most of the time, we don't even realize we're doing it because our intentions are good. We aren't trying to make them mad.

We love them and just want to help.

I think communication breakdown is one reason we begin to assume the mom role. Remember when I mentioned, "If I say it again, maybe you will finally get it"? Any of us who have young children are used to repeating things. Sometimes we don't even know we are doing it. Other times, we do it intentionally because it's the only way we can get through to them.

The communication requirements for being a great mom are not the ones for being a great wife. If we repeat (nag) in hopes that our husbands will listen, our efforts to be helpful can become counterproductive. Repeated telling makes a man feel like a child and puts us in a role that's already taken.

I was shocked and somewhat defensive when my husband reacted to my willingness to share my opinion for the tenth time by saying, "You're not my mom." I wasn't trying to be. He's got a mom, and an awesome one. What I wasn't seeing was the way my husband was interpreting my need to help. Here's something I learned that day: He heard me the first time. I didn't need to make my point ten times. I bet your husband hears you, too. His actions may not show it, but he has to decide what he's going to do on his own. You are not responsible, as a mother is to her child, for his actions, even if you feel his behavior is childish. Say something only once because the more we say it, the closer we come to being the dreaded nag. What we can do repeatedly is pray that our husbands will seek God and that we will have the strength to be suitable helpers for them as their wives, not their mothers.

Consider a mother-in-law's point of view:

Not giving "bossy" mom instructions to my son when I have been doing so for more than two decades isn't easy. And heaven forbid that my daughter-in-law should be tempted to fill that instruction gap. I'm praying God will help her and me see him as mature, fully capable of gathering needed input and making great decisions.

Be the daughter-in-law you hope to have:

- Give your opinion only once. He heard you the first time.
- Pay attention to the things his mother does that he doesn't like for her to do. Steer clear of those behaviors when you interact with your husband.
- Pray for God to guide your husband.
- Pray for God to help you do your part in supporting him.

"Want him to be more of a man? Try being more of a woman!"
—COTY PERFUME AD

Your Husband Is Not Your Dad

Know therefore that the LORD your God is God; he is the faithful God,
keeping his covenant of love to a thousand generations of those
who love him and keep his commandments.
DEUTERONOMY 7:9 NIV

Our relationships with our dads will impact our relationships with our husbands. So it is good to think through what issues we are more likely to have simply because of our upbringing. In our marriages, we can choose to break generational cycles. What we don't want to be passed on to our children, and then to their children, doesn't have to be passed on. We can choose a better way and not do life in default mode. Through the power of Christ, we can be the generation that starts a thousand generations of blessing. It is not easy. It is a daily effort, but it can be done.

Maybe you aren't dealing with generations of frustration or dysfunction. A few things can still trip you up as a wife, even if you had the best father in the world. For example, if you had the joy of being a "daddy's girl," that's not a bad thing at all. As a result, though, you may be tempted to expect your husband to measure up or to be just like your dad. Have you ever thought or said to your husband, "My dad would never do that"? Yes, I am guilty of that, too! I am ashamed to have muttered those words, and regret it. I can't imagine what my husband was feeling at the time. My guess is belittled, hurt, frustrated, and inadequate. After all, I didn't marry my dad; I married him. God created my husband especially for me, and yours for you. If we learn to appreciate the unique gifts that God has given our husbands, we value and love them for who they are and not what we want them to be. They will feel respected, loved, and supported by us, their biggest fans.

It's possible that you had a dad who was physically present, but not emotionally available. Or perhaps you had no father figure at all. You may face the temptation of expecting your husband to fill that void or role. He can't. That's a role he will never be able to fill, and you should not expect him to because that was not the assignment God gave him. People are not perfect, and we will get disappointed and hurt. God is the only One who can and will fill that void. He is waiting and willing to be that Father in your life.

Consider a mother-in-law's point of view:
My daughter-in-law is wonderful, and I hope my son tells her that often. I compliment her, but affirmation from a mother-in-law doesn't touch her heart the way a word from her husband can.

Be the daughter-in-law you hope to have:
* Honor your father by honoring your husband.
* Look at who your husband is, not at who he is not. Your husband is not your daddy, and if you are looking at who he's not, you can't see who God created him to be.
* Share your family history with your mother-in-law so she can understand where you are coming from.
* Pray that any dysfunction that has plagued your family for generations can end with you.

> *"Success in marriage does not come merely through finding*
> *the right mate, but through being the right mate."*
> —BARNETT R. BRICKNER

Your Husband Is Not Your God

Do not put your trust in princes, in human beings, who cannot save.
Psalm 146:3 NIV

Some of us attribute nearly superhuman powers to our husbands without even realizing we are doing it. It's hard to imagine that a wife would put her husband in a god category, but remarkably, there are a few ways a wife might do just that. When a wife says to her husband, "Why should I have to tell you? You should know how I'm feeling" isn't she implying that she believes he can read her mind and intuitively understand her deepest feelings? When a wife goes with the silent treatment because "he ought to know what I'm thinking and feeling," she attributes to her husband a godlike omniscience.

The reality is no man is omniscient. Ninety percent of husbands, ninety percent of the time, (these are approximations) have no clue we are even giving them the silent treatment, let alone a clue of what we are thinking about. They don't understand what it is like to be a woman and generally are glad they don't. We are so different from our men. We have about a trillion raging hormonal issues that we deal with all the time. I need a tissue just thinking about it.

Now that we have all come to our senses and realized just how ridiculous it is that we would try to get our men to read our minds, let's move on to another godlike requirement we give our husbands—rescuer. A personal example: Early in our marriage, we moved to Cincinnati and both got good jobs. My plan after work one day was to ride the bus home with a friend. I had to stay later than expected, so she went on without me. I thought I could catch the last bus out that day, but got the schedule mixed up and ended up missing the bus.

Stranded downtown, I called my husband, who was with a friend playing a round of golf. He asked if I could take a cab home. "Take a cab?" First of all, I didn't see any cabs in the ghost town I was in, and secondly, what I needed was for him to come get me. Somehow he was missing that. Our priorities clearly were not lined up that day. I reacted strongly to his unwillingness to volunteer to come and get me, and that frustrated him. I was crushed that he would not leave to save me. He was angry that I expected him to drop what he was doing as if it weren't important.

I realize now that my request for a ride was not out of line. And Josh didn't think it was out of line even at the time, which is why he offered the solution of a cab. It was the expectation I had placed on him to rescue me in the way I wanted to be rescued that was out of line. But at the time, no option offered was good enough for me because I wanted him to be the one to save me. I wanted him to meet me in my distress and rescue me from what I was imagining.

The good news is that we don't need for our husbands to be our god. We just need them to be our husbands. We have a God—a real God, who loves us unconditionally. And He wants us to have a personal relationship with Him. When we accept His offer of salvation, we discover that the relationship we have with Him impacts every other relationship we have.

Consider a mother-in-law's point of view:

I hope my daughter-in-law will embrace the differences between the way she and my son think and consider them an asset to their marriage.

Be the daughter-in-law you hope to have:

- Communicate with your husband when you want him to know what you are thinking. He cannot read your mind.
- Prioritize your relationships—put your relationship with God first, your relationship with your husband second, your relationship with your children third, and your relationship with everyone else after that. (These priorities are laid out in Proverbs 31.)
- Avoid making decisions while you are scared or upset. Unless it is a life-or-death decision, wait until you are thinking rationally.
- Look to God to save you from spiritual and emotional disasters.
- Pray that your mother-in-law will trust you to love her son, your husband, well.

"A perfect wife is one who doesn't expect a perfect husband."
—AUTHOR UNKNOWN

Chapter Eight

Tackle Insecurities

—Lisa Hunter

INSECURITIES. EVERYBODY has them. Everyone struggles with them. Why are they so difficult to overcome?

Who of us has not occasionally thought, "I'm not good enough," or has not feared being too inadequate to handle a task? Everyone experiences moments of insecurity, but some struggle with it on a daily basis. Those with lingering insecurities, who feel unaccepted or rejected by others, may be nearly devastated by them. Such thoughts unchecked can become strongholds that keep us from becoming the people God intended us to be.

Our insecurities can keep us from having healthy relationships and give us the crazy idea that isolating ourselves from others is a solution to feeling bad about ourselves. As you might imagine, a mother-in-law is not likely to know what to do to build a relationship with a daughter-in-law who is scared and isolated. Just the same, we wouldn't know what to do if that situation were reversed and our mothers-in-law were dealing with such insecurities. If we let our insecurities dictate our lives, we sabotage our own happiness, see ourselves as victims, and often blame those closest to us for "making us this way."

I know I don't want to live like that. And I can't imagine you would want to live like that either. God doesn't want us to establish our lives on our insecurities. He desires for us to be free from every stronghold. God, who is Himself a relationship—Father, Son, and Holy Spirit—made us for relationships, including a relationship with our mothers-in-law.

There are a few steps we can take on the road to a healthy relationship with her and others. Simple ones like praying and studying God's Word are bound to help us make progress. We find our security in God and we learn about Him as we spend time with Him and find out what Scripture says. We can't love well until we know we are loved well. Additional steps toward healthier relationships may be to seek professional counsel or have a mentor speak into our lives. Some of our insecurities could stem from childhood and may require more than we can do for ourselves. Word of warning: once the process begins it will cause temporary discomfort. Things may seem to get worse before they get better. Once we decide to get healthy, watch out!

There is an enemy of all God's goodness who will do everything in his power to keep us from making progress. Satan wants nothing more than for us to falter, give up, and quit. But don't lose heart, as "the one who is in you [God] is greater than the one who is in the world [Satan]" (1 John 4:4). When we experience adversity, we are doing something right. Our good choices threaten him. Being vulnerable, learning to trust, and seeing ourselves in the way that God sees us takes time. Don't get discouraged by the time factor. Seeking God daily and repeatedly turning insecurities over to Him will help you overcome them. You can do it!

It's important to realize that when we feel inadequate or fearful and choose to isolate ourselves, we're not the only ones who feel that way. My father-in-law is a pastor, and I heard him say in a sermon, "Never underestimate anyone's insecurities." I think about that a lot. It's so true. Everyone is insecure, even mothers-in-law.

If you are dealing with a difficult mother-in-law, there is a real possibility that she's difficult because she's insecure. That may be hard to imagine, but remember, she's not the only woman in her son's life anymore. That alone can open up feelings of inadequacy and intimidation, and she may feel replaced and not needed. I encourage you to remember my father-in-law's words, and never underestimate even your mother-in-law's insecurities. As we think about what life looks like from our mothers-in-law's perspectives, being kind to them gets easier. When our hearts soften toward them, our compassion and love for them grows.

Let's look at some of the ways a daughter-in-law can deal with insecurities that have their roots in demands, despair, or fear.

Deal With Demands

I am not commanding you, but I want to test the sincerity of
your love by comparing it with the earnestness of others.
2 Corinthians 8:8 NIV

Over the years, I've heard many women complain about their demanding mothers-in-law. More than one mother-in-law has belittled her daughter-in-law, "Why is your house so messy?" Others insist that daughters-in-law should have dinner on the table when their husbands get home from work each evening. And it's not unusual for a mother-in-law to say to the mother of her grandchildren, "You need to get better control of your children." I'm sure you, too, have heard women complain about similar comments that they've heard from their mothers-in-law.

And there are other types of demands some make that we may not immediately recognize. At first, they seem so positive. For example, mothers-in-law who want to be helpful to their daughters-in-law and "will not take no for an answer." Or mothers-in-law whose sole purpose in life is to be their daughters-in-law's very best friend. Or mothers-in-law who want to "spoil" their grandchildren, believing they have the authority to override what we, as moms, have said should be done. These kinds of demands are all too familiar to many women.

If you are dealing with a mother-in-law who is demanding, there are a few things that can be helpful to consider. First, remember God made her. It helps to think of her as a person who is making demands, rather than labeling her. In other words, try not to refer to her as a demanding mother-in-law. She is so much more than her demands. When you handle her demands instead of trying to "handle" her, you will be better able to deal with each issue individually and still love her as a person.

Aubrey is one of those women on the receiving end of a mother-in-law's critical demands. Every time she and her mother-in-law are together, Aubrey ends up frustrated with her. Her husband's mom, Mary, harasses her. If the kids leave toys on the floor, Mary makes a passive-aggressive remark like, "You must not be home a lot." And when it comes to the topic of cooking, Mary is always quick to lecture Aubrey on how she did things when Dave was living "at home." You can imagine the frustration Aubrey feels. Or maybe you don't have to imagine it because your mother-in-law is a lot like Aubrey's. Maybe you, have felt like pulling your hair out. When your frustrations escalate to that point, here's the truth: You're allowing her to control you. This is unlikely to happen if you handle her specific concerns, as annoying as they might be, and keep your focus on doing what God needs you to be doing.

The second thing to do when addressing a specific demand of your mother-in-law's is to tell your husband what the issues are and your plans for handling them. Make sure your words and tone steer clear of making him feel like he needs to defend his mama. Avoid using phrases like, "I hate it when your mom . . .," or, "Your mother is a crazy lunatic," or, "She's creepy, and I can't stand being around her." Words matter, and presentation is key. Your husband may have some great ideas about how you can keep from offending his mother while accomplishing your goal of reducing her demands. He's a great resource, but don't assign him the role of middleman between you and his mom. You are a capable adult, and when you have not only your own and your family's best interest at heart, but his mother's as well, you are ready and able to deal with her directly.

On the flip side, there are mothers-in-law who make no demands of their daughters-in-law—seriously, none. But for whatever reason, perhaps paranoia, or maybe a need to fit in with others who have mothers-in-law that are quite demanding, some daughters-in-law makeup repulsive traits about their mothers-in-law. They just assume their mothers-in-law live to direct them. As much as it might simplify a daughter-in-law's life to see her mother-in-law through the lens of stereotype, it's wrong. And why would we choose to walk on eggshells because we feel pressure to fulfill unrealistic expectations that we are pretty sure she has. It's sad, but it happens. When we fear what we imagine our mothers-in-law might be thinking or we assume that they are trying to make us miserable, we miss them. We totally and completely miss who they are.

Consider a mother-in-law's point of view

My son's wife doesn't do things the way I do. It's difficult to know how to be a mom to a son who is no longer a child. And it's even harder to know how to be a good "mom" to a daughter I didn't raise.

Be the daughter-in-law you hope to have:

- Give your mother-in-law the benefit of the doubt. Try to see the best in her.
- Try to see the world through her eyes. Remember, she knows she's not the only woman in your husband's life anymore.
- Make an effort to spend time with her.
- Keep the lines of communication open. Talk it out. Talk through issues from your heart. Conversations can take away the unknown and alleviate insecurity.
- Pray for her. And watch what God does with your heart.

"Discover beauty in everyone [even your mother-in-law]. If you've got it in you, get along with everybody [including her]. Don't insist on getting even; that's not for you to do. 'I'll do the judging,' says God. 'I'll take care of it.'"
ROMANS 12:17B-19

Leave No Room for Despair

As I sink in despair, my spirit ebbing away, you know how I'm feeling, know the danger I'm in, the traps hidden in my path. Look right, look left—there's not a soul who cares what happens! I'm up against it, with no exit—bereft, left alone. I cry out, God, call out: "You're my last chance, my only hope for life!" Oh listen, please listen; I've never been this low. Rescue me from those who are hunting me down; I'm no match for them. Get me out of this dungeon so I can thank you in public. Your people will form a circle around me and you'll bring me showers of blessing!
PSALM 142:3-7

Taylor always hoped for a great relationship with her mother-in-law, Jackie. In the early months of Taylor's marriage to Ryan, Jackie was somewhat distant from her daughter-in-law. Taylor hoped they would become closer, and she tried to build a relationship with her, but Jackie kept her distance. After a couple of years had passed, Ryan's parents ended their thirty-year marriage. Taylor knew Jackie was hurting, and once again tried to reach out to her. But Jackie chose to remove herself from the family by moving away. She didn't tell anyone where she was. Taylor and Ryan committed to each other to be there for Jackie if she ever returned, but they needed to stop searching for her and put her into God's hands.

Many months had gone by without any communication from Jackie when out of the blue, Taylor and Ryan discovered that Jackie had moved into a house in their neighborhood! Taylor's heart opened, and she prayed that God would give her the courage to pursue Jackie without expectation.

She decided to write a letter to Jackie to let her know how much she and Ryan loved her and missed her. That relationship grows stronger day by day because a daughter-in-law refused to let her mother-in-law's despairing situation stop her from caring.

Maybe you have tried many times in many ways to reach out to your mother-in-law, but have been ignored or given the cold shoulder. Like Taylor, you may have sincerely desired to have a great relationship with your mother-in-law but discovered that's not something you can make happen by yourself. Eventually, even the most tenacious of us will give up. Before we do that, we might want to think about the reasons she's choosing to keep her distance. Is there something going on in her life that she doesn't want you to worry about, a huge burden that she might not want you to have to help her carry? Maybe she would love to have a closer relationship with you, too, but her reasons for avoiding one may prevent you from ever knowing that.

When we feel rejected, our natural response is to retreat and stop trying. And certainly we don't want to bother the very ones we are simply trying to love well, so after we have tried various ways to involve our mothers-in-law in our lives and were met with little or no response, we need to do what Taylor did—remain available, but let it go for a time. There will be future opportunities to try to connect with her. A woman who won't respond to her son's wife is dealing with some type of issue. It's unfortunate both that she is carrying her lonely burden and that her daughter-in-law is burdened with regret because she can't know what is driving her mother-in-law away. If this is your situation, don't give up, but be wise in how you will deal with this.

God never gives up on us, but neither is He always chasing after us. Much of the time, He gives us reminders that He is waiting for us to decide to come to Him. In that, He gives us a wonderful example of how to love well. Even if a mother-in-law seems cold, unlovable, or unreachable, a daughter-in-law's faithfulness, patience, and prayers can open ways for God to work in her heart.

We continue to shout our praise even when we're hemmed in with troubles,
because we know how troubles can develop passionate patience in us,
and how that patience in turn forges the tempered steel of virtue,
keeping us alert for whatever God will do next.
ROMANS 5:3B-4

> We need to love our mothers-in-law without expectation.

Besides the ones mentioned previously, there are other reasons our mothers-in-law might be tempted to keep their distance. For instance, if they believe we are interested in building a relationship with them for our selfish gain, they may choose to stay away. Trying to connect with them only to get something from them is wrong. We need to love our mothers-in-law without expectation. Let's check our intentions. A need for free child care or a desire to be named in their wills isn't a worthy foundation for a relationship with them. Motives must be unselfish because if they sense otherwise, then putting up boundaries and keeping their distance from us might be their best choice.

Let's pray that we will have pure hearts and good intentions toward our mothers-in-law, and that, as much as it is up to us to be able to do so, we make no place for despair in our relationships with them.

Consider a mother-in-law's point of view:

I'm not trying to frustrate my daughter-in-law, but I have so much responsibility and am dealing with issues that I don't really want to share with her. My problems aren't her problems. I know she prays for me, and that's what I need right now more than I need a conversation.

Be the daughter-in-law you hope to have:
- Be careful not to generalize because of a specific incident or issue. Just because she's not responding in a certain situation doesn't mean she doesn't care.
- Take the lead. Don't wait for her to take the first step.
- Do your part. Love without expectation.
- Don't give up if there's little response to your efforts.
- Pray for a pure heart in your relationship with her.

> *"When you feel like giving up, remember why you held on*
> *for so long in the first place."*
> —Unknown

Remove the Fear Factor

> *God is love. When we take up permanent residence in a life of love,*
> *we live in God and God lives in us. This way, love has the run of the house,*
> *becomes at home and matures in us, so that we're free of worry on Judgment Day—*
> *our standing in the world is identical with Christ's. There is no room in love for fear.*
> *Well-formed love banishes fear. Since fear is crippling, a fearful life—*
> *fear of death, fear of judgment—is one not yet fully formed in love.*
> 1 John 4:17-18

With insecurity comes fear—fear of failing, not being loved, or not being good enough. At the core of all of our insecurities—being rejected, not being accepted, or feeling inadequate—is fear.

Fear puts us in a defensive position and limits us to responsive roles rather than initiating ones. As we get focused on defending ourselves rather than looking for ways to take our relationship to a higher level, our fears will grow. Our fears can be a roadblock in or the demise of our relationships with our mothers-in-law. There are daughters-in-law worldwide who fear they cannot measure up to their mothers-in-law's expectations. Some daughters-in-law are just flat-out scared to be around their mothers-in-law, thinking, What if I do or say something she won't approve of? These fears are prevalent worldwide. There is even a word for the fear of one's mother-in-law: pentheraphobia.

This phobia is not just moments of nervousness that we experience with our mothers-in-law. When I met my mother-in-law, I was very excited and was nervous at the same time. And there have been occasions over the nearly two decades that I have known her when I was a little tense about how she would respond to this or that. But being apprehensive sometimes, about a specific conversation or issue, is normal. In fact, it is a sign the relationship is healthy. These kinds of emotions indicate we know we are interacting with a real person whose response, whether positive or negative, is valuable to us. But if we are actually scared of her, our fear will not allow us to value the person or her response.

> Good connections with our mothers-in-law cannot happen if we fear them.

Pentheraphobia is an issue throughout this world, but it does not need to be an issue for us. Let's think through a few ways to keep it out of our lives.

There is a Japanese proverb that says, "Fear is only as deep as the mind allows." That is so true! When fears and doubts creep into our thoughts, we don't think rationally. So before we know it, our imaginings can cause us to fear things that don't exist or haven't happened. Living scared is not fun.

I heard something recently that makes sense to me, and it helped me get a better understanding of why we fear. The comment was, "Love is the opposite of fear. You have likely always heard that hate is the opposite of love and bravery is the opposite of fear, but those are only surface opposites. There is something deeper, more profound, than that: Love is fear's opposite." It's so true! We cannot love someone who scares us. Good connections with our mothers-in-law cannot happen if we fear them.

Scripture tells us there is no fear in love (1 John 4:18). And God is love (1 John 4:17). Therefore, God has no fear. God is never scared. (If that isn't the best evidence that the opposite of love is fear, I don't know what is.) So when we find our personal security in Christ, and we begin to trust Him with our fears, our ability to love well grows. When we invite God to take away the fear we find we are experiencing in any of our relationships, including pentheraphobia, He will.

Consider a mother-in-law's point of view:
I wish I knew how to make our relationship more comfortable, but even an uncomfortable relationship is better than no relationship at all.

Be the daughter-in-law you hope to have:
- Memorize 1 John 4:18: "There is no fear in love. But perfect love drives out fear, because fear has to do with punishment. The one who fears is not made perfect in love."
- Recognize you can't love your mother-in-law well if you fear her.
- Decide to take the risk—do not isolate yourself from her, even when you are afraid.
- Try to communicate your fears to her.
- Pray for God to take away your fears and replace them with His love.

> *"FEAR is an acronym in the English language for*
> *'False Evidence Appearing Real.'"*
> —N. D. WALSCH

Chapter Nine

Keep the Big Picture in Mind

—Rhonda Hunter

Having a great vision for your relationship with your mother-in-law gives perspective to daily interaction and makes any conflicts you have with her easy to address appropriately. A great vision for your relationship gives you a platform not only to bless each other but also to inspire others and significantly impact the generations yet to come. God brings people together for His purposes, but we can choose to ignore what He has in mind. Proverbs 29:18a warns us that if we ignore His noble intentions, there will be problems: "Where there is no vision, the people perish" (KJV).

Years ago, at a dinner at Summit Church in Orlando, where my husband serves as senior pastor, a speaker encouraged all couples in attendance to create a mission statement for their marriage. He told us that a marriage "has to be about more than just the two of you." My husband, Isaac, and I had made several promises to each other—we would never argue about any hypothetical issues, we would never consider divorce to be an option, and so on—but we had never boiled our marriage down to one statement of what we wanted our lives to be about. So we met the challenge and came up with our mission statement: "To honor God by the way we love each other, our children, and the people around us."

I want my marriage to be bigger than the two of us, and I want my life to be about more than just me. I want all my relationships to be affected and influenced by my decision to follow Christ. Of course, that includes my relationship with my mother-in-law. Fortunately, she has the same desire. But even if she didn't, I would want my understanding of the bigger picture, the greater vision, to benefit her and the rest of our family.

Keep Details in Perspective

Casting down imaginations, and every high thing that exalteth
itself against the knowledge of God, and bringing into
captivity every thought to the obedience of Christ . . . .
2 CORINTHIANS 10:5 KJV

In every relationship, perspective is critical. Keeping the big picture, or the "grander vision," for the relationship in mind affords you the opportunity to keep the everyday details in perspective. If you don't have any greater vision than day-to-day convenience, you will inevitably make mountains out of molehills. And your relationships will fall far short of their potential.

A few years ago, my husband and I took our kids to Disney World for the day. We had a great day. My son, Lincoln, was twenty months old at the time. He loved it, until the very end of the day, when he wanted a football with Mickey's face on it. The football retailed for approximately $17,000. We didn't buy it for him. There was no consoling him from that point forward.

It was the only part of the day he was denied anything his little heart desired. But it was all he could concentrate on. I tried to explain to him how great a day he had enjoyed, but it was useless. He couldn't see the whole day. One part had blotted out the big picture.

I didn't blame him for being upset. After all, you can only require so much perspective from someone who has yet to celebrate his second birthday. I wasn't expecting him to embrace my argument as to why he should see this incident as a minor inconvenience in the light of a really wonderful day.

My husband and I try to help our kids see every frustration and disappointment in light of the bigger picture. It's crucial for their ongoing development and maturity. It is for ours, too.

As we mature, our perspective enlarges. We are able to see rough patches as what they are—they are patches—not "the way things will always be."

If you go through a difficult time with your mother-in-law, put it in perspective. You passed two a long time ago, so make your maturity count for something. She gave you her son, and if that's not consolation right now, remember that God gave you both of them to love. Don't let small things blot out the big picture.

Having a workable relationship with your mother-in-law is a good thing, but it's not the only end you are striving for. Ultimately, that end is honoring God, and blessing your husband, your children, and the people your family has the potential to influence.

Don't waste time and energy getting caught up in wishing things were different, hoping things will get much better than they are. Start where you are in your relationship with your mother-in-law, and work forward from there. Think about how you would approach her if you had never met her. What would your countenance be? What tone would you use with her? Start fresh from right where you are today, and work toward God's will for your life. God may not change all the circumstances immediately, like you wish He would, but He will change you, and ultimately that changes everything.

Consider a mother-in-law's point of view:

I love that my daughter-in-law isn't afraid to dream big. I'm on my knees for her and will help her any way I can as she extends herself for Kingdom purposes. My son married well. I need to remember to tell him that.

Be the daughter-in-law you would like to have:

- Write a vision statement of how you want your relationship with your mother-in-law to be.
- Do not let comparing rob you of the joy that can be found in what you've been given. If you notice other family members getting nicer gifts, more babysitting time, or other general perks, resist the urge to get upset. Put yourself in her shoes, and realize that it's hard for your mother-in-law to distribute all her free time and money equally. You don't automatically deserve these things. They are gifts from her, and sometimes, whether you

like it or not, they go to the neediest first.

- Try to find the positive in the situation. There is almost always one to be found. Always assume the best rather than imagine some mean underlying message in her words or actions.
- Pray for an accurate perspective as you interact with your mother-in-law.
- Choose not to make mountains out of molehills. If it is a huge deal, then say something about it. If not, let it go.

"A little perspective, like a little humor, goes a long way."
—ALLEN KLEIN

Model Relationships for Next Generations

We're not keeping this to ourselves,
we're passing it along to the next generation—
God's fame and fortune,
the marvelous things he has done.

He planted a witness in Jacob,
set his Word firmly in Israel,
Then commanded our parents
to teach it to their children
So the next generation would know,
and all the generations to come—
Know the truth and tell the stories
so their children can trust in God,
Never forget the works of God
but keep his commands to the letter.
PSALM 78:4B-7

Where did you first learn what it looked like to be a wife? Where did you learn how to deal with conflict? How about what God must be like? Our first lessons about almost everything came from watching the generations before us: our mother and father, grandmothers and grandfathers. Whether those lessons were mostly right or mostly wrong, they were powerful.

Those early lessons can be unlearned if they need to be, but from personal experience, I can say we are better off when the right lessons were modeled from the beginning. My mother has repeated to me over and over since I was a little girl, "You're the daughter of the King, and He made you to do amazing things in this world." Now I find myself repeating the same thing to my girls.

In relationships, we want to be good examples for our children. We want to be good examples for our nieces and nephews. We want it enough to work toward it and pray for it. But I suppose the pertinent question in this moment is, do we want it badly enough to invest our time and energy to model what it means even to love a mother-in-law well?

Our relationship with our in-laws lays the foundation for our children's future relationship with their in-laws. If your children see you doing everything you can to treat their grandparents in a God-honoring way, that standard will bless them and their families decades from now.

Consider a mother-in-law's point of view:

Each passing year gives more clarity to the importance of each decision I've made and action I've taken. I pray that I can keep in mind the number of years it took to get that clarity, and that I can share my insights in a way that never weighs down, but always inspires, the generations that follow.

Be the daughter-in-law you would like to have:

* Go with a good attitude when your in-laws invite you to their home.
* Always speak well of your mother-in-law.
* Invite your mother-in-law to your family's events, but don't get frustrated if she can't come. It's an invitation. Your part is asking; not judging her response.
* Pray for strength and wisdom to live your life in a way that will benefit generations to come.

"Whoever teaches his child teaches not a lone child, but also his child's child, and so on to the end of generations."
—HEBREW PROVERB

Inspire Others to Reach for God

Therefore go and make disciples of all nations, baptizing them in the name of the Father and of the Son and of the Holy Spirit, and teaching them to obey everything I have commanded you. And surely I am with you always, to the very end of the age.
MATTHEW 28:19-20 NIV

It may seem a bit odd, and even a little self-important, to think that you or your family can be an inspiration to others, but it is true. You were made to make an impact, and make no mistake—your life will make an impact one way or another. The future direction and scope of that impact are yet to be determined.

You may not think of it that way all the time, and that's okay; most of the time, we should just be about doing the next right thing. But every once in a while, it is good for us to note the role our actions play in shaping other people's lives. We have both the responsibility and opportunity to inspire others simply by being faithful.

No one can deny the impact of love lived out well. We've all seen it. Sometimes we are fortunate enough to see it up close.

I will never forget Grandma K or as she was known by most, Ruth Katauskas. We weren't family by blood, but my sister Kelly married her grandson Eric. It didn't matter to her that she wasn't actually my grandmother or my children's great-grandmother; she treated us like family. She quickly became Grandma K to us. Her sweet life marked her family and still does. And it marked my life and the lives of my daughters.

Grandma K had a way of making everyone feel special. When we attended family gatherings, she invited my girls to sit with her at the piano, and taught them how to play and sing songs about Jesus. She never looked past them. She always made them feel important. Her impact spanned generations and her amazing love continues to inspire and bless the people who knew her.

You don't need to be perfect. No one but Jesus ever has been. But your husband and your family members, your friends, and the world need you to be the kind of person who is striving to live the kind of life you are inviting other people into. You can't do anything to earn Jesus' love, but once you understand how much He loves you, you can be very intentional about reflecting that love to other people.

You have the ability to follow Jesus in such a way that your life inspires others toward love and good deeds, to reach for Him. The way you determine to treat your mother-in-law in every season of life will influence and potentially inspire others. The same goes for her, but you can't control her, and you won't be held accountable for what she does. You do the best you can with what you've got, and God will honor that every time.

My mother-in-law often says, "You can lead others toward Christ or away from Him. The choice is yours." That's it! What will you choose?

Consider a mother-in-law's point of view:
When my daughter-in-law goes out of her way to be kind to me, I am blessed by that, and I know that her efforts are not impacting me alone. Every kindness observed in our relationship can and often does inspire others.

Be the daughter-in-law you would like to have:
- Think about the fact that your life can inspire others.
- Thank the people who are inspiring to you.
- Do the next right thing. If you aren't sure what that is, try asking yourself, "What would Jesus do?"
- Pray that your attitude and interactions honor your mother-in-law in ways that honor Christ.

Our life is full of brokenness - broken relationships, broken promises,
broken expectations. How can we live with that brokenness without
becoming bitter and resentful except by returning again and again
to God's faithful presence in our lives.
— Henri Nouwen

Endnotes

1. Film: Monster-in-Law, screenplay by Anya Kochoff, 2005.

About the Authors

LISA HUNTER

Lisa Hunter's favorite things in life are being a wife and a mother. The Hunters married in 1996. She and Josh have two children: a son, Noah, born in 1998, and a daughter, Ava, who was born in 2004 and at five years old battled brain cancer for ten weeks and moved to Heaven on September 4, 2010. Since going through the journey of cancer, with Ava, Lisa has become a passionate voice of encouragement for alternative medicine and healthy lifestyle whether dealing with cancer or everyday life. Lisa accepted Christ as her personal Savior when she was 11, and ever since that time, she has loved to encourage people God puts in her path. She majored in music at Bryan College in Dayton, Tennessee and taught piano for years. She has used her love of music and her education to serve as a children's ministry worship leader, not only in the United States, but also in Argentina as a part of a church training outreach. She is very supportive of Josh, in his role as CEO of Hunter Vision, a 3D LASIK provider in Orlando, Florida.

Contact Lisa Hunter:

Hunter Vision
8701 Maitland Summit Blvd.
Orlando, FL 32810
www.huntervision.com
E-mail: lisa@whyher.org

RHONDA HUNTER

Rhonda Hunter met and married Isaac in 1999 (when you know, you know). She finds great joy in being mom to their children: Jada, born in 2001; Ella, born in 2003; and Lincoln, born in 2007. Rhonda accepted Christ as her personal Savior at age five. Her compassionate nature led her to earn a Bachelor of Science degree in psychology at Rollins College in Winter Park, Florida. Her studies required a semester in Europe. After graduation, The Center for the Homeless in South Bend, Indiana, hired her to serve as a social worker. During that time, she assisted Isaac on weeknights and weekends in his ministry to the middle and high school youth of Granger Community Church. Now, back in Central Florida, she leads a weekly Bible study and volunteers her time in her children's schools and several community organizations. Rhonda is very supportive of Isaac in his role as senior pastor of Orlando's dynamic multi-campus Summit Church, which they planted in 2002.

Contact Rhonda Hunter:
Summit Church
735 Herndon Ave.
Orlando, FL 32803
www.summitconnect.org
E-mail: rhonda@whyher.org

ELIZABETH HUNTER

Elizabeth Hunter met and fell in love with Joel in 2006 and the two were wed in 2007. She loves being mother to their son, Luke, born in 2009. Elizabeth became a Christian when she was just three years old. After many years pursuing musical studies, she went to college at Palm Beach Atlantic University and earned a Bachelor of Music degree in vocal performance. In the following years, she performed in various venues including a two-year stint as a resident artist with the Orlando Opera Company. She has traveled extensively, spending time on five continents engaged in various study and mission efforts. She has ministered to children through Awana Clubs and has taught voice and piano to people of all ages. Elizabeth is very supportive of her husband Joel the founding ophthalmic surgeon of Hunter Vision, a 3D LASIK provider in Orlando, Florida, founded in 2010.

Contact Elizabeth Hunter:
Hunter Vision
8701 Maitland Summit Blvd.
Orlando, FL 32810
www.huntervision.com
E-mail: elizabeth@whyher.org

Why Her?

YOU, YOUR DAUGHTER-IN-LAW,
and the BIG PICTURE

BECKY HUNTER

Acknowledgments

I am grateful to God for the privilege of writing this book and for other blessings too numerous to count. And I am thankful for the support and encouragement that my incredible husband, Joel, offered me throughout this project.

My heartfelt appreciation goes to Lisa, Rhonda, and Elizabeth Hunter, the godly women my sons married. I love them as I would if they were my own daughters. The relationship we share is what inspired the writing of this book. What a privilege it has been to work together with them these past three years on *Why Her?*

Thanks go to my sons, Josh, Isaac, and Joel, who must have quietly wondered why their own mother would take on a project that would require their wives to meet deadlines and be even busier than usual. These amazing men I thank God for every day.

Thanks go to Michele Graves, my sister-in-law, and Sandy Graves, her daughter-in-law, who took time when we began this project to help us think through important dynamics of the mother-in-law/daughter-in-law relationship.

My sincere appreciation goes to Melissa Bogdany for her professional edits, to Tracy Weiss for the layout and cover designs, to Dede Caruso for additional formatting, to Josh Hunter for author photographs, and to Robert Andrescik for his encouragement and for walking us through the publishing process.

Thanks go to the hundreds of women who have shared with me their personal stories and insights about mother-in-law/daughter-in-law relationships.

And last, but not least, thanks go to the pastors' and elders' wives of Northland, A Church Distributed for praying for all of us as we wrote.

Why Her?

YOU, YOUR DAUGHTER-IN-LAW,
and the BIG PICTURE

BECKY HUNTER

WHY HER? You, Your Daughter-in-Law, and the Big Picture
by Becky Hunter

ISBN 978-0-9786783-3-3

Dedication

I dedicate this book to the godly women who raised my incredible
daughters-in-law: Patty Gable, Lisa's mother; Kim Hauser, Rhonda's mother;
and Shirley Ariza, Elizabeth's mother. Thank you from the bottom of my heart
for living faith-filled lives, which inspired your beautiful daughters
to fall in love with Jesus, too.

Contents

Introduction

AT LUNCH ONE day in a hotel with her son Reggie and his new wife, Gloria, Alice Vanderbilt asked whether Gloria had received her pearls. Reggie replied that he had not yet bought any because the only pearls worthy of his bride were beyond his price. His mother then calmly ordered that a pair of scissors be brought to her. When the scissors arrived, Mrs. Vanderbilt promptly cut off about one-third of her own $70,000 pearl necklace and handed the pearls to her new daughter-in-law. "There you are, Gloria," she said. "All Vanderbilt women have pearls."[1]

When we give what we value, not only do we honor the one to whom the gift is given; it also helps us value that person more. As Matthew 6:21 says, "Where your treasure is, there will your heart be also" (KJV). We may not have a string of pearls to hand to our daughters-in-law, but each of us has a string of valuable resources—prayers, ideas, encouragements, and meaningful items— that we can give to our daughters-in-law to let them know they matter to us.

This book is more about why we should invest in our daughters-in-law than how to do that. It is a "why to" book more than it is a "how to" book. Each situation is unique, so how to be a blessing to your daughter-in-law is something you will have to figure out on your own, but it is impossible to figure that out if you don't know why a good relationship with her matters.

Our primary responsibility when it comes to our daughters-in-law and our sons is to encourage them toward God and each other. This is seldom accomplished by instruction. More helpful is understanding their unique situation and then offering whatever "pearls" we possess.

Chapter One

Connect Two Families

YOUR RELATIONSHIP WITH the woman your son loves can become a high-light in your life. Whether you find your daughter-in-law's values and points of view to be points of connection or hurdles to leap, it's important to keep in mind that your daughter-in-law had parents who shared more than their genetics with her. They shared their values, traditions, and idiosyncrasies with her for many years as she was growing up, just as you and your husband shared yours with your son. While you were busy raising your son, another woman was busy raising her daughter, and on the couple's wedding day, your two families are joined in aspects that future generations will bear out in myriad ways. No doubt about it, when the couple becomes one, they aren't the only ones who are embarking on a new adventure.

Congratulations! You Are a Mother-in-Law!

Therefore shall a man leave his father and his mother,
and shall cleave unto his wife: and they shall be one flesh.
GENESIS 2:24 KJV

When you hear your son say, "I do," it's hard not to cry. That's true whether you are happy for him, or sad, or fearful, or angry about his choice for a wife. Whatever the reason for your emotional state, the tears are evidence of the significance of the moment. You know there are few, if any, more important decisions that your son will make in his lifetime than choosing a woman to be his wife. And somewhere deep in your soul, you know that a change in your relationship with him is inherent in his marriage vows.

Whatever the reason for your wedding tears, it is time to archive your mental images of his boyhood and to begin picturing him as a mature adult with a primary responsibility of being a great partner to his wife. Updating your image of your son, seeing him as her husband and not your little boy, will give you the best possible vantage point from which you can begin to be a blessing to both him and her.

A few years ago, I was chatting with Melanie Stockstill, a pastor's wife whom I greatly respect. She asked me if any of my three sons were married. At the time, only our son Josh was married. I told Melanie how blessed I felt to have Lisa, the long-awaited "daughter," in my life. Melanie, also a mother of sons, said she enjoyed the women her sons had chosen to marry. I asked her if she had any tips to share about being a good mother-in-law, as she had more years of experience in that role than I did.

> When our sons marry, we should transition from hands-on to "hands up" and celebrate that God loves to meet their needs.

Her wise response: "I had more than twenty years to love on my boys. My sons know I will love them always, but now they 'belong' to their wives. So I have made it my goal to love on their wives for the rest of my life."

Building a good relationship with the woman your son loves may not be easy, but it is easy to see in Melanie's choice a way to make it wonderful. Melanie chose to love. We can choose that, too. Ask God to give you that kind of heart for your daughter-in-law. He loves your son's bride, and He will help you love her, too. And what better day to ask God to give you that love for her than the day they say, "I do."

I've been a pastor's wife since 1972 and have attended hundreds of weddings. Some grooms' moms make fascinating choices. I've seen them:

- choose to miss their son's wedding. ("*Wouldn't I just be giving my*

blessing to his poor choice for a wife?")

- undermine a future daughter-in-law with "helpful instructions" about what the wedding—and, in fact, everything else—should look like. (*"One day she will be so glad this wedding was done right."*)
- try to hold a son's attention, distracting him from his bride. (*"This is my last real day as his mom; she will have him for the rest of his life."*)
- walk out of the ceremony. (*"I thought I could do this, but I can't. I just can't."*)
- cry so loudly that the guests were focused on her throughout the ceremony (*"I've always been emotional."*)

Besides these, and perhaps most startling, I witnessed a groom's mom get out of her seat and adjust her son's tux vest as his bride was coming down the aisle.

There is a common thread in these moms' behaviors. They dread losing the role of "first lady" in their sons' lives. Their boys are now men with loving wives, and the moms sense a "forced retirement" in the air. And if the term "mom" is limited to the hands-on, "I can fix this for you" stage of life, then indeed, their jobs are over. But that's not the case. "Mom" doesn't have term limits. We moms can continue to bless and encourage our sons, and also our sons' wives, by lifting their needs in our prayers. When our sons marry, we should transition from hands-on to "hands up" and celebrate that God loves to meet their needs. May we never underestimate our value as conduits of God's love for them as we bring their needs before Him for the rest of our lives.

Consider a daughter-in-law's point of view:
I love her son so much I'm marrying him. Shouldn't that be enough for my mother-in-law? What else should matter?

Be the mother-in-law you wish you had:
- Honor your daughter-in-law by not looking more like a bride than the bride herself—no whiter whites, no greater gown, and certainly no eye-popping cleavage. This is HER wedding day.
- Guard against stealing your son's attention from his bride, even for a moment.
- Remember how stressful a wedding day is for a bride. Plan to let nothing your daughter-in-law says or does on her wedding day stand in the way of

your building a great relationship with her.

- Make sure you tell her how beautiful she looks.
- Pray for your son's wife—it's the first day you will have that opportunity.

"Even though I had let them do things since babyhood like choose their own socks, I was only beginning to learn to trust their adult judgment. I had a sensation very much like the moment in an airplane when you realize that even if you stop holding the plane up by gripping the arms of your seat until your knuckles show white, the plane will stay up by itself. To appropriately detach myself from my adult children, I had to achieve a condition that might be called loving objectivity."
—Anonymous

Build Family Traditions

God can do anything, you know—far more than you could ever imagine or guess or request in your wildest dreams! He does it not by pushing us around but by working within us, his Spirit deeply and gently within us.
Ephesians 3:20

In the musical *Fiddler on the Roof*, Tevye and the other villagers of Anatevka sing about traditions at a place where and time when every person's role in life was dictated by tradition. In Tevye's world and sometimes in ours, traditions give family members strength and stability, a sense of certainty in what it means to be family.

Tevye and his wife valued tradition more than almost anything, and maybe you prize tradition that highly as well. That's nice. But when your son gets married, quite frankly, the chances of your family traditions matching perfectly with his wife's family traditions are next to zero. So, do your son and daughter-in-law a great favor, and let them combine, alter, remove, or add traditions so that they will get the greatest sense of certainty about what it means to be family.

I watch mothers-in-law struggle with the notion that "if only 'the children' (a description struggling mothers-in-law seem to prefer over 'my son

and his wife') understood how important this is to me, to us as a family, then they would carry it into their new life together." It doesn't occur to these women that their "children" probably do under-
stand. When something holds the status of family tradition, it's pretty obvious that it matters to you. But just because they understand that you cherish a tradition doesn't mean they will or should em-brace it as a couple. And if you choose to remind them of its importance to you, essentially forcing them to carry it into their future together, you are likely to see it played out grudgingly. Undue pres-sure and piled-on guilt often produce results, but the results are typically temporary and are never

> Tradition all too easily can switch from being an historical aspect of a family to being the hysteri-cal requirement of a family.

pretty. And because they aren't, you'll find yourself tempted to try to adjust "the children" yet again.

When Joel and I were raising our sons, one of our family traditions was to travel to Ohio every summer and spend a week with extended family. When the boys were young, the five of us piled into a compact car in Orlando and piled out of it twenty-two hours later on the shores of Lake Erie. Stopping at pancake houses, reading Bible stories, playing the alphabet game in the car, and reminding one another for about the last eighteen hours of the drive that we were almost there were all part of the tradition. In later years, driving was replaced with flying, but the destination, the tenacity it took to get us all there together, and the resulting joy of that remained unchanged.

Traditions are a blessing when they build a family story line rather than create expectations for every future generation. Joel and I still make the trip to Ohio every summer, and some years our sons, their wives, and their children all get there, too. However, sometimes they don't. And while, obviously, our preference is to be with them as we participate in this annual event, whether they make it there or not, I'm so grateful Joel and I had the opportunity to build that tradition from the time of our sons' early childhood, and I'm grate-ful that now they have opportunities to build their own traditions.

Tradition all too easily can switch from being an historical aspect of a family to being the hysterical requirement of a family. While we know traditions cul-tivate connection among immediate family members and among generations, we may not stop to think how honoring the choices of our sons and their wives

as they establish their own traditions can accomplish that same goal. When it comes right down to it, you are going to have to decide if the traditions you cherish matter more to you than to the very family that they were meant to strengthen. That valuable comfort and closeness that you discovered through the tradition you've embraced all these years can be lost forever if the tradition trumps the comfort and closeness it was meant to establish. How many mothers-in-law damage relationships with a daughter-in-law solely because a cherished family tradition has been laid aside by a son's wife?

The most important traditions are the ones based on God's commandments and a commitment to a personal relationship with Him. Prayer, worship, study of the Bible, fellowship, and helpful service are among the traditional aspects of faith that orthodox Christians practice. These religious traditions have real value, though, only if the person practicing them really believes that God is who He says He is. You can't give your faith to the next generation via traditions. Every person has to receive a gift of faith directly from God. So, as valuable as they are, determining even to push Christian traditions onto your son and daughter-in-law is useless, unless your goal is limited to the practice of the rituals themselves. And what is the logic of that endgame? Hopefully you have modeled, and continue to model, through the way you live your life the personal relationship you have with Christ. A disciplined and joy-filled life gives testimony to the value of personal faith, and real meaning to the traditions you cherish.

Consider a daughter-in-law's point of view:
Doesn't my mother-in-law remember that she created the traditions with her family that she wants me to carry on? I really just want the same opportunities she had to create traditions with my husband that will strengthen our family.

Be the mother-in-law you wish you had:
- Start a new tradition, one that is designed specifically to bless your daughter-in-law.
- At appropriate times, and without expectation of a specific response, talk to your daughter-in-law about the family traditions that have meant something to you personally, and ask her to tell you about some of the meaningful traditions that her family cherishes.
- Evaluate the traditions you've incorporated into your life, and if there are

some that no longer serve the purpose that they are intended to serve, let them go.

- Make a scrapbook or photo album of the traditions you had in your home while your son was growing up. (Memories keep well in such formats, and when a grandchild flips through the pages someday in the future, he or she may be inspired to reinstate traditions lost to his or her parents' generation.)
- Pray for a perspective that welcomes the future more than it longs for the past.

"Traditions are the guideposts driven deep in our subconscious minds. The most powerful ones are those we can't even describe and aren't even aware of."
—Ellen Goodman

Holidays: Rituals of Reassurance

God's love, though, is ever and always, eternally present to all who fear him, making everything right for them and their children as they follow his Covenant ways and remember to do whatever he said.
Psalm 103:17-18

When I was in seventh grade, it was cool to have people write quips on and sign notebook covers. Sitting in class one morning, I was reading the various words of wisdom my classmates had written on mine, and I noticed a brand new entry. At some point in the previous twenty-four hours, unbeknownst to me, my dad had "borrowed" my notebook and penned: "Be a good girl today so that all the special days will be special. Love, Your Dad." At the time, I just thought it was weird that my dad would write on my notebook, but over the years, that tidbit of wisdom saved me from making lots of poor choices, and to be honest, it still does.

Only when normal days are rightly lived can days designated as special really be special for us. That insight is beneficial to us in all of our roles:

daughter, sister, wife, mom, and mother-in-law, just to name a few. Specific to our topic, it's very difficult for a holiday to be an awesome experience between a mother-in-law and a daughter-in-law if they are warring throughout the rest of the year. Our choices are to build the relationship along the way, or prepare ourselves for the trauma that will be intrinsic to our times of celebration.

Families have varied traditions of holiday celebrations, but I think it is safe to assume that most families in the United States make some effort to come together on either Thanksgiving or Christmas, or both.

By Thanksgiving each year, we had sufficiently recovered from our summer vacation travels to Ohio and again stuffed our boys into our tiny car and drove one thousand miles to Indiana, where I grew up, in order to celebrate a Thanksgiving-Christmas holiday with my extended family. "Thanksmas," as we called it, was a holiday tradition that continued long after our sons had families of their own, but eventually ever more complicated aspects of getting everyone together caused us to move Thanksmas from Mom's house to our memory banks.

Thanksmas celebrations were possible because we held to the heart of a tradition in a nontraditional format. If you have conflicts with your daughter-in-law concerning your family's holiday traditions, consider some ways you could hold on to the heart of traditions you value while graciously relinquishing the exactitude you prefer.

Sometimes the best holiday experiences are found in a pre- or post-holiday event.

The year was 1997, and Christmas was just around the corner. Our oldest son, Josh, was a student at Taylor University in Indiana at the time, and his fiancée, Lisa, was teaching music in Orlando. I enjoyed Lisa, but didn't know her prior to Josh's dating her. We were able to spend very little time together because between her schedule and mine, free time was scarce. So I was pleasantly surprised that afternoon when she showed up at our front door with a box of Godiva chocolates. I shoved aside the papers I was grading, and we chatted over the box. It wasn't long before half the candy was gone and we had so much sugar energy that we decided to put up our Christmas tree together. I think that day was the day we bonded.

We retrieved the freshly cut pine tree from the garage, where it had been leaning against a wall for the past few hours. We were wrestling that big,

prickly pine into the tree stand, and as we were trying to tighten the screws of the tree stand, that tree toppled and fell on top of us, pinning us to the tile floor. Sprawled there, peeking at each other through the pine needles, we laughed until we were almost sick. (Looking back, I blame the Godiva chocolates more than the hysteria for the wooziness I was feeling at the time.) Here's the point: I remember that Christmas prep fun more than anything else about that particular Christmas. Are there ways you could make pre- or post-holiday times extra special? Tapping into the anticipation that surrounds most holidays is a great way to relieve some of the undue pressure associated with such special events.

Consider a daughter-in-law's point of view:
How is it that a specific date on the calendar can be so critical to my mother-in-law's believing I care about her? I feel like some kind of a celebration hostage.

Be the mother-in-law you wish you had:
- Don't tie your thoughtfulness and generosity to having your expectations met. Real gifts don't have strings attached.
- Check with your daughter-in-law in advance of holidays, and ask if she and your son have any time on those special days that you all could get together. If your plans are not flexible, then simply invite her and him to join in your festivities, making it clear it is an invitation, not an expectation of their participation. Coerced participation in a holiday activity is more likely to build walls than bonds.
- Be really okay with any effort your daughter-in-law makes to be with you on a specific day. She's got two sets of "parents" to please. A half day with you means only a half day with her folks; celebrating a holiday with you every other year means she doesn't see her parents every other year on that holiday.
- Consider celebrating a holiday on a day different from its calendar date. For example, celebrate Christmas December 26, have Thanksgiving on Friday rather than Thursday, or celebrate everyone in the family's birthdays on one designated day and make the whole day a party.
- Ask your daughter-in-law if you can assist her in any way before or after a holiday get-together.
- Pray that when your family does have opportunities to be together, your

contributions to the gathering will include joy and kindness.

"The joy of brightening other lives, bearing each other's burdens, easing others' loads, and supplanting empty hearts and lives with generous gifts becomes for us the magic of the holidays."
—W. C. JONES

Love Your Daughter-in-Law's Husband

WE KNEW WHAT was required to be a good mom for a boy, but the characteristics of being a good mom to the man he has become can elude us. If we are ever going to love our daughters-in-law well, we have to figure out how we can love well the married men that our precious boys have become. What are the characteristics of a good mom to a now married son? A threefold, but partial, answer to that question is: a commitment to show them respect, honor their choices, and love their wives. Beyond that, to love them well, we have to make good decisions about what we are going to do with the rest of our lives.

All those years we invested our time and effort into them, making sure they ate right, got enough rest, studied hard, and grew in their relationship with God, are now history. Ironically, moments we remember so vividly are randomly distributed through days that felt like lifetimes and years that flew by. Whether time stands still or flies by, how we spend it matters forever. Every season of life matters, and in this season, like every other, we consider what matters to our sons' well-being. One thing we can do to love them and their wives well is put effort into caring for our own physical, mental, and spiritual health.

Love Him by Taking Care of Yourself

Don't you realize that your body is the temple of the Holy Spirit,
who lives in you and was given to you by God? You do not belong to yourself.
1 CORINTHIANS 6:19 NLT

You and I surely did our best to help our sons build strong, healthy bodies. And good for us—that was a great gift to them. Now we can give them another great gift by doing our best to stay healthy ourselves. Every day that we don't give our sons or their wives something to worry about we give them a gift. Let's do what we can to stay healthy, if not for ourselves, then at least for our families.

So many women in their sixties, seventies, and eighties look great, stay active, and are proving that aging is mind over matter. If we don't mind, it doesn't matter! This is the time in our lives when we can tackle a project we never were able to set aside time to get to, devote ourselves to volunteerism, or step into positions of leadership that a lifetime of focusing on the needs of others has prepared us to do well. At this stage, we have a wealth of real life experience to offer. So we are downright startled to discover, just as we have these wonderful things to offer to our families and the world, our bodies didn't get the memo that it's time to be awesome.

Random aches and pains remind us that we must be intentional about caring for our bodies. Exercise used to be an option, but it's no longer optional—now it is a requirement. Being a supermodel isn't the goal; being a role model is. If we are active, we'll find that our bodies remain flexible, and our moods, steady.

Strenuous workouts were part of my teen sons' everyday routines. And since Joel and I had sold all of our dining room furniture and replaced it with weights and other gym equipment, it wasn't like I couldn't have lifted a barbell now and then myself. But I didn't—I just thought about it. Instead of bonding with them over weight benches, I decided to bond with them over a kitchen table. That would have been fine, except for all the tempting food that was on it. I'm embarrassed to say, I matched my juvenile athletes bite for bite at most meals. The quality of food was fine, but the quantity, not so much; I

just didn't need that much food! But it was there, it was yummy, they were there, they were fun to talk to—and, well, you get the picture. The only other place we had such great relaxed conversation time was in the car as I ferried them from home to school to church to practices.

When we have married sons, our daily schedules are no longer built around family meals or taxiing sons to activities. Many of us in this season of life find it easier than ever to be disciplined with our eating and diligent about exercising. And that occasional nap we longed for is within the realm of possibilities!

With the day-to-day stress of raising our sons now a thing of the past, we can investigate our options and take on whatever we've thought we might like to do if we could make the time. Living each day in a way that shows our sons and their wives that growing older has advantages is a good thing to do. At the very least, it helps them not worry about us, and at its best, we might even inspire them. Now we can donate our time to church and community efforts that will make life better for others, and maybe we can take a trip we always dreamed about. This stage of our lives has no fewer blessings than previous stages. We just have not had reason to consider our current blessings before now. I still remember a lighthearted comment made to my mom when she first became an empty-nester. A friend who had two married sons said, "Wandah, there's nothing that says boys are grown and gone better than laying white carpet in your house."

If we maintain disciplines in our lives that provide us with good health, and we strive for just even a kempt appearance, our sons and daughters-in-law will have even more reasons to really enjoy staying close to us for the rest of our lives. And their closeness will keep our hearts healthy in ways that exercise can't.

Consider a daughter-in-law's point of view:

My mother-in-law never fails to point out ways I "jeopardize" my husband's health, yet she eats junk, gets no exercise, and says it's her time to enjoy life. What's that about?

Be the mother-in-law you wish you had:
- Pray for a long, healthy life so you can use it to bless others.
- Practice a disciplined life; master your body so you can be most effective in working toward God's purposes in your family and community.

- Educate yourself on how to keep your body healthy in this postmenopausal season of life.
- Save your discussions about your aches and pains for your doctor. If you have important health issues your son and his wife should be aware of, then, of course, tell them, but generally speaking there are plenty of things to talk about with your son and his wife besides your health.

"The only exercise some people get is jumping to conclusions, running down their friends, sidestepping responsibility, and pushing their luck!"
—Anonymous

Love Him as an Intellectual Pursuit

Who gives intuition to the heart and instinct to the mind?
Job 38:36 NLT

In the early 1970s, a college funding initiative introduced a very catchy tag line for use in its advertising: "A mind is a terrible thing to waste." That blunt truth is probably one you've heard before. It's a sentiment that impacted the diligence with which I taught my sons. And now, as their senior years of high school and even college are long past, I contend with a different kind of "senior moment." I need to be diligent about my own mind not going to waste.

Minds are the seedbeds of our attitudes and actions. Where does our thinking come from? How much of it is of good quality? How much of it is of poor quality? How much of our thinking is muddled, illogical, or superficial? We need to know because good, clear, logical, and well-considered thought is critical if we are going to maintain a meaningful relationship with our married sons.

When my sons were young, I often, really often, reminded them, "Garbage in, garbage out." Good-quality thinking has always required high-quality input. We had minimal disagreement about the truth of that statement, but oddly enough, my definition of garbage and the boys' definition of garbage weren't always identical. Once we got beyond the objective words of Scripture,

there seemed to be a sense of subjectivity when it came to almost any other subject that at times was downright annoying. Even if it was hard to distinguish garbage on the intake, it was easy enough for everyone to recognize it on the output. Bad attitudes and gross actions don't come to life in a vacuum; they are birthed in our thoughts.

The Scripture encourages us: "Fix your thoughts on what is true, and honorable, and right, and pure, and lovely, and admirable. Think about things that are excellent and worthy of praise" (Philippians 4:8, NLT). What is the purpose in that? The answer is found in the next verse. We are to think on wonderful things so that we will put such godly things into practice and God will be with us and we'll experience peace.

What kinds of things do you consider when you think about your son and his wife? As you ponder the various aspects of their lives (their personalities, dreams, children, jobs, and so on), can you picture each facet in light of the encouragements of Philippians 4:8?

I'll give you an example of what I mean. Our oldest son, Josh, and his wife, Lisa, have very different personalities. Josh is goal-oriented and very content to work alone for hours to accomplish a task at hand, while Lisa is very relationship-oriented and views accomplishment in terms of the lives she can touch. That's just the plain and simple truth. And it is always important to recognize a truth. Once I discover such a truth, I can focus on what is admirable and excellent about the unique way that God has made each of them and how key their personalities are in helping them to accomplish together what God intends. When I use the grid of Philippians 4:8 in such a way, my perspective becomes more like God's, and it becomes easy to praise differences.

Our thought life will make or break the relationship we have with our sons and daughters-in-law.

Consider a daughter-in-law's point of view:

When my mother-in-law is reasonable, it really doesn't bother me even if we have a difference of opinion. But when she speaks out of her baseless fears or without any understanding of the facts, conversation is unpleasant at best.

Be the mother-in-law you wish you had:

- Pray for a thought life that keeps you focused on the best and helps you

cherish the good as you develop your relationship with your son and his wife.

- Use Philippians 4:8 to guide your thinking and keep it focused.
- Check your words and actions as you interact with your son and daughter-in-law. If those words and actions are negative, figure out what garbage you are taking into your life, and cut the flow.

"Educating the mind without educating the heart is no education at all."
—ARISTOTLE

Love Him With Your Very Soul

God, your God, will cut away the thick calluses on your heart and your children's hearts, freeing you to love God, your God, with your whole heart and soul and live, really live.
DEUTERONOMY 30:6

Our eternal identities reside in our souls. So when Jesus stated there is no commandment more important than to "love the Lord your God with all your heart and with all your soul and with all your mind and with all your strength" (Mark 12:30, NIV), He let us know that souls have been designed to love.

The obvious and most significant aspect of the Great Commandment in Mark 12 is that to love God well, we need to use every resource we have been given to its maximum. Every resource He mentions is prefaced by the admonition to use "all" of it in order to love Him well. His Great Commandment lists our souls among the four capabilities that we possess that allow us to love. Scripture is clear: We are to love God and love people with all our soul.

How do we do that?

We do it by loving them through every season and every stage of existence, both in the now and the hereafter. Maybe that's why so many mothers find it easier to love their sons forever than to love almost anyone else for even a day. Moms are so keenly aware of their sons throughout the many stages of their

lives—from the moment of conception to adulthood, our souls know, love, and value our sons.

Surely, our eternal souls' capacities to love are infinite. All of the other ways we have been given to love, through our hearts (emotions), minds (intellects), and strength (bodies), impact our souls. The soul is not an isolated source of love. It is enriched by the other three sources in ways that make its infinite nature exceptionally valuable for Kingdom purposes.

As our sons progress through the stages of life, the specific ways we have of loving them, the expressions of our love that will most benefit them, shift among those seats of love that Jesus mentioned: heart, soul, mind, and strength. Loving costs us physically, mentally, and emotionally, but it replenishes our soul. Let's review, for a minute, how the various seasons of our sons' lives affected our lives. Let's look at some of the changes we made along the way in order to love them well.

When moms are fully engaged in their rightful parenting roles, they are exhausted. Seriously, I don't know a woman raising great kids—aka training up a child in the way he should go—who isn't tired, nor do I know any such mom who is raising great kids whose soul is void.

The kinds of exhaustion that mothers experience through the various stages of child rearing correspond to the ways in which we have been equipped to love. Remember the physical exhaustion so commonly experienced when caring for the youngest among us. It is physically challenging to engage daily with a baby or a toddler, and perhaps the ultimate physical challenge is a preschool boy.

Moms of infants rally to a new day by announcing on Facebook, "I got to sleep four hours straight. He didn't wake up until almost 4 A.M. today!" And once babies become toddlers, we verbalize our exhaustion by reminding ourselves and others that they are doing a lot of exploring and are too young to understand that it is not safe to "crawl up on the cabinet," "stick the plug in that socket," or "throw sticks at people." Then, when the toddler has matured to a preschool-age boy, even if we only take into consideration the number of times in one day we had to repair what he did with the intention of "helping" and the trips we made to check on him in "time out," we are going to feel tired—but our souls will feel full.

Physical wear and tear takes a backseat throughout the next step of parenting, when our young students are learning stuff we haven't thought about for decades or, worse, have never even heard of at all! In this stage, exhaustion is

mental. We are investing in these boys with our whole minds, trying to "stay ahead of," or at least "on top of" the vast amount of knowledge they are gaining daily. If we are making sure our students are where they need to be, when they need to be there, and are adding to what they are learning in ways that encourage and inspire them to be the men God created them to be, our minds feel almost numb—but our souls are invigorated.

Eventually, the mental clarity returns, and moms of teens turn their focus to loving with all of their hearts. Most of the critical input has been given, and moms begin to slowly, very slowly, turn over the controls of their boys' lives to the men they are becoming. That's hugely important, hard work for a mom, and emotionally draining. It exhausts us emotionally—but our souls overflow with love.

When we have poured out our lives so that our sons could grow strong physically, mentally, and emotionally, our souls are enriched, and our sons are blessed. They are men our daughters-in-law will have every reason to love.

Consider a daughter-in-law's point of view:
I wish I could see into my mother-in-law's soul. But since I can't, I choose to live as though I have looked into it and what I saw was beautiful.

Be the mother-in-law you wish you had:
*   Pray that you will sense encouragement for the seasons you invested well into your son, and pray that God will touch your son and heal memories of the seasons when you didn't.
*   Pray that your daughter-in-law will know that you did your best with what you knew when you were raising your son and that you will do the best with what you know now.
*   Consider what your soul has to offer for God's Kingdom purposes, and don't be afraid of the exhaustion that comes with pouring out your life for others in efforts that help them mature in Christ. This is the indicator of a life conformed to Christ. It is the way you love with your soul.

"What can you ever really know of other people's souls—of their temptations, their opportunities, their struggles? One soul in the whole creation you do know: and it is the only one whose fate is placed in your hands."
—C. S. LEWIS

Chapter Three
Just Be Kind

SOMETIMES CLARITY COMES through an antonym rather than a synonym. For example, if I want to make sure someone understands what the word kind means, I could offer synonyms, words that have similar meanings, to give that clarity. Through words like nice, accommodating, and helpful, most people would have at least partial understanding of what the word kind means. But it is in its antonym that we discover a real understanding of what it means to be kind.

What is the opposite of kind? Mean, cruel, and inconsiderate are terms that seem to answer that question. They certainly aren't wrong answers. An answer that offers more clarity, though, is found in the Catholic catechism. The catechism includes lists of the seven deadly sins and their opposites, the seven heavenly virtues. When the lists of virtues and sins are juxtaposed, you won't find meanness, cruelty, or inconsideration opposite kindness. You will find envy. The juxtaposition of kindness and envy is found in 1 Corinthians 13:4 as well: "Love is patient, love is kind. It does not envy, it does not boast, it is not proud" (NIV). Envy isn't just wishing you had what someone else has. Envy despises another person's advantages, accomplishments, and position.

Ephesians 5 tells us that kindness is a fruit of the Holy Spirit. A Christian woman filled with that kindness would not be envious of her daughter-in-law. But what if you aren't filled with kindness? What if you do struggle with envy

and wish your son prioritized your needs over his wife's, or feel he owes you as much as or more than he owes her, or are generally frustrated with what you believe to be your daughter-in-law's advantages, accomplishments, or position? If such is the case, then being kind to your daughter-in-law is going to require you to have a change of perspective, and that will require effort. A decision to be kind to your daughter-in-law is a decision to begin to bless her. You can minister to her through your intentions, encouragement, and trustworthiness.

Good Intentions: Just the Beginning

If the power of sin within me keeps sabotaging my best intentions, I obviously need help! I realize that I don't have what it takes. I can will it, but I can't do it. I decide to do good, but I don't really do it; I decide not to do bad, but then I do it anyway. My decisions, such as they are, don't result in actions. Something has gone wrong deep within me and gets the better of me every time.
ROMANS 7:17-20

It takes a godly perspective, some resources, and disciplined action to give even our best intentions real value. Good intentions are not a substitute for action. It's been said that no one would remember the Good Samaritan if he had only possessed good intentions; he is remembered because he met the need.

If my intention is to be kind to my daughters-in-law, but I never say anything to encourage them or do anything to help them, shame on me. If my intention has shifted entirely from how I can be a blessing to my daughters-in-law to how I can justify myself, greater shame on me.

The Thaindian News, in September 2008, reported on 500 mothers-in-law who have joined forces to embrace their mother-in-law role and polish their image. The article reads as follows:

Indian mothers-in-law have decided to go for an image makeover as they form a union to improve their public image.

About 500 mothers-in-law recently met in Bangalore demanding their rights and campaigning for a change in their public image, which has been marred in the wake of a string of torturous murders of some brides.

Mothers-in-law have often been portrayed as callous, sadistic and dictatorial women who wield unbridled authority over their daughters-in-law. However, the All India Mother-in-law Protection Forum (AIMPF) rubbishes all such allegations.

Given that news, you may be thinking your daughter-in-law is more blessed to have you in her life than even you realized! But before we offer ourselves kudos because torturous, murderous intentions likely have not entered our minds, even on our very worst days, we need to acknowledge that there may be a desire, an intention, to take authority over our daughters-in-law that is not so removed from our thinking.

Years ago, I gave one of my daughters-in-law a gift. She said she liked it, but she never used it. I found myself first pondering her truthfulness (Did she really not like it?) and then silently questioning her gratitude (Was she intentionally disrespecting my kindness?). My thoughts led me to pull my son aside and ask why he thought she wasn't using the gift. His reply: "Mom, did you really mean it to be a gift, something to bless her, or did you give it with strings attached? If it had strings, you should have told her that upfront."

Hmm . . . a genius fellow, my son.

His response brought me to grips with my real and pathetic motives for giving. They were decidedly less altruistic than I had admitted to myself! As I took his words to heart and examined my intentions, I realized I really had expected my daughter-in-law to respond in a way I desired rather than any way she wished. I was trying to get something for me rather than just give something to her. It was a very aha moment in my life. I found in that event a better way to bless not only my daughter-in-law, but also everyone who has received a gift from me since. Anything I give has no strings attached. Now I realize, intention untangled from expectation increases joy immensely.

Consider a daughter-in-law's point of view:
I can only assume my mother-in-law's intentions by what she says and how she acts. I wonder what she assumes my intentions are, given my words and actions around her.

Be the mother-in-law you wish you had:
- Pray that your intentions will be pure. God reads your heart.
- Give a gift with no strings attached.
- Back up your good intentions with appropriate use of your resources (time, effort, and finances).

"We judge others by their behavior. We judge ourselves by our intentions."
—IAN PERCY

Offer Encouragement

Speak encouraging words to one another. Build up hope so
you'll all be together in this, no one left out, no one left behind.
I know you're already doing this; just keep on doing it.
1 THESSALONIANS 5:11

We named our sons Joshua, Isaac, and Joel, but I probably should have named one, or perhaps all, of them Barnabas. That moniker would have been perfect for my sons because I think I was born to encourage. It's my favorite thing to do, and as Acts 4:36 points out, "Barnabas" means "son of encouragement." Technically speaking, anyone who has been tagged with the name Barnabas deserves to have at least one very encouraging parent.

Obviously, you don't have to be named Barnabas to require encouragement. My husband, Joel, often says, "Never underestimate anyone's insecurities." Every person has them. So even if your daughter-in-law appears to be confident and bold, insecurities of one sort or another have found a home in her heart—just like they have found a home in yours and in mine. The good news is encouragement is an antidote for insecurities.

Guess who is strategically positioned to encourage our daughters-in-law well? We are. With a bit of effort, we can encourage our sons' wives in ways that will grow their confidence and build up our relationship with them. As we do this, it is important to remember, encouragement includes neither hidden

agenda nor flattery! Encouraging them to get them to do something we want them to do is manipulation. Trickery like that will fail them and us. And flattery has inherent duplicity; it is flimsy compliment filled with our need to be liked. Flattery will weaken our relationship with them, but heartfelt encouragement will strengthen it and also strengthen them personally!

When we encourage our daughters-in-law, we are pouring courage into them, and the annoying insecurities they deal with every day are drowned out for a time. There are so many facets of their lives that we may admire: their faith, strength, attitude, intellect, discipline, culinary skills, way with our sons, and parenting skills. Commenting on such highlights can build their confidence. And let's not be reluctant to put in a good word about our daughters-in-law when we are with family or out in the community. If they hear we have been speaking well of them to others, or if on some occasion they happen to overhear us saying good things about them to our sons or others, we will encourage them in ways they will never forget.

If offering encouragement has not been your forte—if you are at a loss as to how or what to do to encourage your daughter-in-law—there is a simple technique you can apply to help spur ideas. Simply think of things that you would have appreciated hearing your mother-in-law say to you! Consider the ways she could have poured courage into you, and use the words and actions that come to mind to start encouraging your daughter-in-law.

When we encourage our daughters-in-law, we are investing in our relationship, not just waiting on change. All too often, as we are giving and pouring into them, we are anticipating the return on our offerings. We may not even be conscious of our expectation of payback, but when we get no, little, or, even worse, a negative response, our immediate, but very damaging, reaction can be to attempt to withdraw what we invested!

Look, it is wonderful if our daughters-in-law are effusive with gratitude for our kindnesses, but the way they choose to respond to us is neither the point, nor any of our business. The more significant issue is how our heart responds to them whether or not they said or did what we hoped. So we return to the powerful challenge of Philippians 4:8: "Fix your thoughts on what is true, and honorable, and right, and pure, and lovely, and admirable. Think about things that are excellent and worthy of praise" (NLT). Such thoughts fill us up so that we can continue to be a voice of encouragement no matter what.

Take the challenge of Philippians 4:8, and apply it specifically to your

daughter-in-law. Always try to find the best in every word she says and every action she takes. Look for the best, ponder the best, and you will be taking a significant step toward being the best mother-in-law she could possibly have.

Consider a daughter-in-law's point of view:
I wish my mother-in-law would take note of some of the things I do right. It would be great to hear an encouraging word from her that didn't include a "helpful" suggestion in the same breath.

Be the mother-in-law you wish you had:
- Pray for a sensitivity to your daughter-in-law's perspective so that you can choose words and actions that will be encouraging to her.
- Go out of your way to learn what encourages your daughter-in-law.
- Send her an encouraging message, via mail, e-mail, text, Twitter, or phone—your communication options are endless.
- Give her a gift certificate for something she would consider a practical help or fun extravagance.

> *"A pat on the back is only a few vertebrae away from a kick in the pants,*
> *but miles ahead in terms of results."*
> —ANONYMOUS

Be a Woman of Your Word

No exceptions are to be made for women—same qualifications: serious, dependable, not sharp-tongued, not overfond of wine. Servants in the church are to be committed to their spouses, attentive to their own children, and diligent in looking after their own affairs. Those who do this servant work will come to be highly respected, a real credit to this Jesus-faith.
1 TIMOTHY 3:11-13

Let's be known for our reliability, determination, and honesty. Let's keep

our word so others know we can be trusted. Trustworthiness means we can be counted on. If we make a promise or a vow, let's do all we possibly can to keep our word, no matter how hard it becomes. That requires making wise decisions about what we are actually able to take on and accomplish so that we don't spend our days guilt-ridden for falling short of our goals, or apologizing for shortcomings. Every day, let's do whatever we have committed to do.

If we want to build strong relationships with others, in particular, our daughters-in-law, this attribute is critical. If they know they can rely on us to keep promises, support and protect the family, tell the truth, and do the right thing, they aren't going to see us as the enemy. Real integrity is inspiring.

If we want our daughters-in-law to trust us, do you think they or we have the greater responsibility for making that happen? We may jump to the conclusion that the first step is for them simply to start trusting, but that isn't the first step; that's the final result of our being dependable. They will count us trustworthy after they have observed our faithfulness to the commitments we make. If we are trustworthy one day, but not the next day, it will be difficult for them to trust us at all. They will learn to rely on us when they sense it would devastate us to let them down.

Like most values of life, trustworthiness is better caught than taught.

Are you a trustworthy mother-in-law? Evaluate yourself:

True or False? *I keep my promises to her; I am a person of my word.*

True or False? *I am reliable; I follow through on commitments I've made to her.*

True or False? *I am honest with her.*

True or False? *I never betray her confidence.*

True or False? *I have integrity in my interactions with her.*

If you are thinking this is a test you would love to give to your daughter-in-law, don't. Like most values of life, trustworthiness is better caught than taught. If this attribute is reflected in your life and in your interactions with her, she may choose to become more trustworthy, too.

Consider a daughter-in-law's point of view:

My mother-in-law is kind enough, but I just can't count on her to do what she says. For example, she says the world doesn't need to know my business, but that doesn't keep her from sharing interesting tidbits about my life with her

friends. She says she'll spend Saturday with my kids, but calls Friday night to cancel if anything at all pops up at the last minute. I like her; I just can't rely on her.

Be the mother-in-law you wish you had:
- Pray for the strength to be trustworthy in all things.
- State your commitments to her plainly so that communication issues cannot mar the appearance of your being a trustworthy person.
- Ask your daughter-in-law if there is anything specific you can do that would allow her to more readily rely on you.

> *"It is mutual trust, even more than mutual interest,*
> *that holds human associations together."*
> —H. L. Mencken

Address the Unreasonable

WHEN WE ASSUME anyone will meet our expectations, or we give our moods priority status, or we make lifestyle choices that ignore God or people, we are being unreasonable, aka illogical, impractical, and/or unrealistic. But most of us think that being reasonable is synonymous with being boring. So we take an unreasoned approach to daily life, presuming on family and friends, following our feelings with wild abandon, and becoming addicted even to things that we dislike. In other words, we create environments where regrets will thrive. As we unwittingly plant seeds of regret, we come to realize that once they have taken root, logical, practical, and realistic thinking becomes increasingly difficult to cultivate.

Being unreasonable tends to give us "the stage" and draw a crowd. While outlandish or audacious interactions may make us the center of attention, making it hard to talk ourselves into a more reasonable approach to life, the fact is, being reasonable does have a more long-term value. Crazy decisions, poor word choices, and ineffective or even inappropriate actions do, though, make for potential theatric development; drama and entertainment tend to partner with decisions made on a whim. Adding to our temptation to step toward goofiness is a sadly common misperception that freedom is found by stepping over boundaries (real or perceived) rather than living life "full

out" within them. Huge determination is required to take action based on convictions of personal faith rather than impulsive whims. Whims hate containment even more than they hate commitments.

It's time to confront our unreasonable expectations, moods, and lifestyles.

Let Go of Expectations

That was my reason for writing a letter instead of coming—so I wouldn't have to spend a miserable time disappointing the very friends I had looked forward to cheering me up!
2 CORINTHIANS 2:3a

Even though I am free of the demands and expectations of everyone, I have voluntarily become a servant to any and all in order to reach a wide range of people: religious, nonreligious, meticulous moralists, loose-living immoralists, the defeated, the demoralized—whoever. I didn't take on their way of life. I kept my bearings in Christ—but I entered their world and tried to experience things from their point of view. I've become just about every sort of servant there is in my attempts to lead those I meet into a God-saved life. I did all this because of the Message. I didn't just want to talk about it; I wanted to be in on it!
1 CORINTHIANS 9:19-23

There are two distinct sides of expectation: what we expect from others, and what we believe others expect from us.

Let's spend a moment considering the "what we expect from others" side. There is a good possibility that long before our sons take wives, we anticipate what our relationship will be like with daughters-in-law. Any expectation we have likely is rooted in the relationship, or lack of relationship, we have had with our own mother-in-law, that additional "mom" we got the day we looked at our groom and said, "I do!" If we enjoy the relationship we have with our mother-in-law, we may consciously or unconsciously assume that the dynamics of that relationship will be mirrored in our relationships with our daughters-in-law. If we think our relationship with our mother-in-law leaves something to be

desired, then we may draft new "scripts" for the relationships we hope to have with our sons' wives.

Some of the most positive women I know have set a wonderful tone that overlaps expectation of the relationship by revising the designations of mother-in-law and daughter-in-law. Vonette Bright, cofounder of Campus Crusade for Christ International, refers to her dynamic son's wife, Kathy, as her daughter-in-love. Lisa Clay, a very gifted pastor's wife I met long before her eldest son married, affectionately refers to her daughter-in-law as her bonus daughter. A woman I met at a conference in England told me she always introduces her daughter-in-law like this: "My son got married and gave me a new best friend."

Some of us sensed blessings when our sons married. Others of us met challenges when they did. Either way, welcoming any opportunities to minister to our daughters-in-law is important; both challenges and blessings create equal opportunities for us to be prayerful. If we are willing to let go of our expectations of our daughters-in-law, they can and will begin to make their way into our hearts.

And that brings me to the flip side of expectations: what we believe others expect from us. There is an old saying, "Never bother wondering what people are thinking about you because chances are, they aren't thinking about you at all." Sorry if that truth hurts your feelings, but it was worth sharing for those of you who are struggling with paranoia about your mother-in-law role.

If we worry about what our daughters-in-law expect from us, let's stop worrying long enough to ask them what, if anything, they hope for in the relationship they will have with us throughout our lifetime. Giving them permission to share their perspectives encourages them to come to us along the way, over the months and years, to speak into our lives, especially as it relates to them and their immediate families. Once we know what they expect, we can decide to ignore, meet, or exceed those expectations, but we can never be afraid of information!

Consider a daughter-in-law's point of view:

I would like to know the ways I can disappoint my mother-in-law before I just stumble into those failures. I'm hoping her expectations of me are few, and may God hold my tongue when I'm the one dealing with unmet expectations. Expectations are land mines in the relationship I have with my mother-in-law.

Be the mother-in-law you wish you had:
- Pray that you will have minimal expectations of your daughter-in-law.
- Take the time to find out what she expects from you.
- Set a tone for the relationship in the way you refer to your daughter-in-law.
- Pray for her every day, and let her know that you do.

"If your manna has to drop straight from heaven looking like a perfect loaf of butter-crust bread, then chances are you are going to go hungry a lot."
—BARBARA BROWN TAYLOR

Control Moods

Just because something is technically legal doesn't mean that it's spiritually appropriate. If I went around doing whatever I thought I could get by with, I'd be a slave to my whims.
1 CORINTHIANS 6:12

Moods just exist. We can't help but have moods, but we are responsible for what we do with them. It's all too easy to shirk our responsibilities and give a mood priority status. Some of us inflict our moods on others simply because we are too weak or not disciplined enough to control them. But some of us have an altogether different reason for inflicting our mood on others. We do it because we have been duped into thinking that being authentic, or "real," has more to do with honoring a whim than honoring our commitment to represent Jesus well in every circumstance. Being authentic has nothing to do with downloading a mood. Relationships are incredibly valuable, so handle a mood carefully, and pray no one gets hurt.

> Relationships are incredibly valuable, so handle a mood carefully, and pray no one gets hurt.

Daughters-in-law have a unique window into our lives. They can see us through our sons' eyes, their viewpoints are a generation younger than ours,

and from their vantage points they can see right through our personal presentations into our real lives. Their various points of assessment are as valuable to us as they are to them. Since the relationships we have with daughters-in-law are long-term ones, our lives can unfold naturally. There is no need for us to give rapid-fire family histories, offer tons of advice, or share personal dreams in a few all-or-nothing moments.

A mood, though, will try to convince us otherwise. Moods are easily recognizable by the following characteristics:

- They are isolating: *"I'm the only one who knows how things ought to be. I'll just handle all of this myself."*
- They are general. Something specific may initiate a mood, but almost immediately upon formation, everything will be equally tainted by it: *"That made me mad. In fact, I'm furious about everything right now!"*
- A mood forces our perception of the world through a singular emotional state, and tunnel vision sadness, or madness, or badness elicits neither a helpful, nor appealing response from others.
- All moods are temporary. As a Jewish wisdom folktale about King Solomon states, "This too shall pass."

We underestimate how our moods impact people and especially how they may impact our daughters-in-law. I was talking to a mom whose daughter had recently married, and she said something that really caught my attention: "Becky, you don't have daughters, but you do have a mom, so this should make sense to you. There is a bond between a mom and her girl, and it doesn't end when she's married. My daughter has been married less than a year now, and one of the most amazing, surprising things that I've noticed since she got married is that she can quote nearly verbatim every word her mother-in-law has said since the day she met her. She cherishes her encouragement and tends to see anything she says that isn't blatantly encouraging as a criticism.

"When she calls me, if she sounds discouraged, I can be pretty sure it's because her mother-in-law was, as she puts it, 'in a mood.' I think if that precious lady, and I say that in all seriousness because she really is a precious lady, knew the impact her every word has on my daughter, she would barely be able to believe it.

"A daughter knows what her mom is going to say; she's been saying it for decades. But a mother-in-law's voice is new and different. I bet there isn't a mother around who believes that her daughter's life won't be impacted for

better or worse by her mother-in-law. I just wish that mothers-in-law would take a moment to think about their impact."

Consider a daughter-in-law's point of view:
I hate trying to guess what kind of mood my mother-in-law is going to be in when I call or interact with her face to face. Honestly, sometimes I feel like I'm dealing with Sybil.[2]

Be the mother-in-law you wish you had:
- Pray for strength to control a mood when it strikes.
- Be understanding when your daughter-in-law is "in a mood." You have had decades of practice controlling yours, so you are doing life with a more mature skill set.
- Prevent moodiness; spend time with God every day, work out, eat right, get rest ... put all those well-known emotion stabilizers into practice.

> *"Life is a train of moods like a string of beads; and as we pass through them they prove to be many colored lenses, which paint the world their own hue, and each shows us only what lies in its own focus."*
> —RALPH WALDO EMERSON

Show Trumps Tell

> *The lifestyle of good people is like sunlight at dawn that keeps getting brighter until broad daylight. The lifestyle of the wicked is like total darkness, and they will never know what makes them stumble.*
> PROVERBS 4:18-19 CEV

Even if our daughters-in-law share our faith, value what we value, and make choices based on what they understand from their study of Scripture, they will make decisions we wouldn't make, and they will do things differently from the way we would do them. If they don't value what we value, and they have no idea what the Bible says, or, even more disconcerting, they

have rejected what it says, we still don't walk away, and we don't try to "fix" them. If our lifestyles are nothing like theirs, they will notice that without us saying a word about it. In fact, anything we say about the way they live will be interpreted as judgmental. Until they can observe us for a long time, see that we are faithful and have hearts of love and compassion, our "constructive" comments are likely to depress, frustrate, worry, or annoy them. We have a lifetime to pray for and encourage these women our sons have chosen to be their wives. And there will be many opportunities over the years that God will give us to love them well. In the meantime, we can pray for wisdom to say what will be truly helpful when those moments come. And we can pray that we won't add to the stresses they feel. (They do feel stress, whether or not we think they do.)

Each of our daughters-in-law is a unique child of God. She is someone who is loved by God and worthy of a place in eternity. I wish the heartfelt desires of mothers-in-law would be to see their daughters-in-law draw close to the Lord and honor Him, and for daughters-in-law to prioritize their marriage relationship and love their husbands well. I'm sure these things are the concerns of many mothers-in-law, but that's seldom what I hear these women talking about. Their comments about their daughters-in-law tend to focus on things that are superficial and subjective, things that should be none of their concern. Here's a random sample of pronouncements of conflicting ideals I've recently heard mothers-in-law express:

> **Each of our daughters-in-law is a unique child of God.**

- *"I wish she had a job,"* or, *"I wish she were home raising the children."*
- *"I wish she cared more about her appearance,"* or, *"I wish she didn't spend their money shopping for herself."*
- *"I wish she wanted to have children now,"* or, *"I wish she would wait to have children until they are more established."*
- *"I wish she paid more attention to my son,"* or, *"I wish she would give my son more time to himself."*

You get the point. No wonder daughters-in-law joke about never being able to please us. They know we have opinions on just about everything, and they know we think our opinions are correct.

The most significant input we have to offer our daughters-in-law is not our words; it is what we communicate through the lifestyle we've chosen and our

faithfulness to live it well. The more our lifestyle honors God and we strive to meet the needs and hopes of others, the more likely our daughters-in-law are to glean something of value as they observe the way we live. For example, if we love our husbands well and honor them in our homes, and love doing that, then over time, as our daughters-in-law observe those interactions, they may decide to love and honor their husbands in some of the same ways. On the other hand, if they see us simply tolerate our husbands, whine about their "expectations," or roll our eyes behind their backs, we surely can't be too surprised when our daughters-in-law disrespect or mock our sons. That old adage is true: More is caught than taught.

Consider a daughter-in-law's point of view:

I wish my mother-in-law realized that I'm not being obstinate. I just don't believe everything she believes, and it frustrates me so much when I feel like she isn't going to be happy with me until my days look just like hers.

Be the mother-in-law you wish you had:
- Pray that you will have the strength to live a godly lifestyle.
- Pray that your daughter-in-law will take note of those things in your life that would benefit her and that she will ignore anything that would not be helpful.
- Make life choices that bless other people.
- Tame your tongue—use words only when necessary.

> *"Be not angry that you cannot make others as you wish them to be,*
> *since you cannot make yourself as you wish to be."*
> —Thomas à Kempis

Chapter Five

Add Insight

I F WE ARE going to have growing relationships with the loves of our sons' lives, we must be adaptable. We are capable of cherishing our daughters-in-law as much as we cherish our own sons, but we are going to have to be intentional about getting to that point. Any less commitment to them than to our sons, and we are scripting our relationship with them with melodrama and disappointment. Faith not only gets us through this time of transition; it generates a desire in us to embrace a future that includes this woman who has captured our son's heart!

Stories of first meetings of mothers- and daughters-in-law are fun to hear. There is no script for that first memorable get-together, and sometimes it is long after the fact that we come to realize that we've met the one who will marry our son! Settings and conversations vary from family to family at that significant meet and greet. But whether we are aware of its significance in that moment or find out that information later, there is a time and place when we see, for the very first time, the woman our son has chosen to be his wife.

Once we know our son is getting married, it makes sense to get all the biblical insights into the mother-in-law/daughter-in-law relationship we possibly can. There may be no better place to look for them than in the book of Ruth.

Walk With God

God's way of putting people right shows up in the acts of faith, confirming what Scripture has said all along: "The person in right standing before God by trusting him really lives."
ROMANS 1:17b

From the book of Ruth, we learn that more than one thousand years before Christ was born, a Jewish woman named Naomi, her husband, and her two sons were starving due to a famine in their homeland of Judah. So they moved. The family set up residence in Moab, a place with a very different culture and different religion.

Sometime after moving to Moab, Naomi's husband died, but she and her sons chose to remain in Moab. Eventually, each of the sons married a Moabite woman. Ten years later, both sons died and left behind young widows, Ruth and Orpah.

Naomi faced serious poverty. Since the famine in her homeland had ended, she made the decision to return to Judah. She started the journey back to her homeland with her daughters-in-law. But then, for reasons that aren't clear, she told her daughters-in-law to stay in Moab, where they could live with their families and eventually remarry. Was Naomi unselfishly placing what she believed to be her daughters-in-law's preferences over her own? Most biblical scholars believe she was. Not surprisingly, though, her daughters-in-law's preferences were not identical. While both Orpah and Ruth wept with her, Orpah went back to Moab, while Ruth insisted that she would never be apart from Naomi and continued with her to live in Judah.

Why did Ruth decide to follow Naomi to a strange land? The only clue we are given in the text is Ruth's simple declaration: "Where you go, I will go, and where you lodge, I will lodge. Your people shall be my people, and your God, my God. Where you die, I will die, and there I will be buried" (Ruth 1:16-17, NASB). Today that declaration of dedication is more likely to be spoken between a bride and a groom. Most people would be surprised to learn the words were spoken by a daughter-in-law to her mother-in-law.

We won't know for sure on this side of Heaven exactly why Ruth chose to stay close to Naomi for the rest of her life, but her words hint at the reason for her decision. When Ruth said to Naomi, "Your God [will be] my God,"

it wouldn't be much of a stretch to assume that Naomi must have honored God with her everyday life in a way that drew Ruth's interest. If Naomi had been obnoxious, overbearing, crabby, wimpy, or in other ways unlovely, Ruth surely would not have given up all that was familiar to be near her.

The book of Ruth gives us enough information that we can infer that Naomi's faith was unchanged by foreign surroundings. She held closely to her faith and modeled a life with God while at the same time giving her daughters-in-law freedom to live according to their culture and understanding. In both good times and bad times, Naomi was an effective witness for God. Had she been judgmental or angry with the women about their religion or their culture, Ruth surely would not have chosen to stay with her when the family obligation to do so no longer existed.

A great insight about faith that can be seen in Naomi's interactions with her daughters-in-law is the importance of living out God's promises. We have nothing to gain and much to lose if we spend time or energy trying to orchestrate changes in our daughters-in-law's lives. Our own faithful, flexible walk with God is what makes for a strong story together.

Consider a daughter-in-law's point of view:
I don't think identical theologies are critical to getting along with my mother-in-law, but she acts like they are. I have no idea what to do about that. I don't just feel like she's judging me; I know she is.

Be the mother-in-law you wish you had:
- Pray that God will fill you with His Spirit, for His purposes, every day. Live a life that demonstrates your faith.
- Resist the urge to preach to your daughter-in-law, and instead find ways to serve, aka minister to, her.
- Let her know you love her enough to give her some distance from you when she needs it—not only geographically, but also emotionally. In other words, don't be afraid to give her some space!
- Be sure your faith is strong and your expressions of it are forever flexible.

"Faith isn't the ability to believe long and far into the misty future. It's simply taking God at His Word and taking the next step."
—JONI EARECKSON TADA

Wait for God's Grip

Blessed is ... the woman who sticks with God. ... like trees replanted in Eden, putting down roots near the rivers—never a worry through the hottest of summers, never dropping a leaf, serene and calm through droughts, bearing fresh fruit every season.
JEREMIAH 17:7-8

Most of us are unprepared for the changes and adjustments that must be made when we go through a transition, but prepared or not, transitions are part of life! You know that. You have experienced a major transition: Your son got married. You can't get to the stage of life where you are a mother-in-law without having experienced times of transition: marriage, children, jobs that came and went, parents' aging, and beloved relatives passing on. You definitely know what transitioning feels like.

Hopefully, our transitions will be fewer in number and come to us through less inherently traumatic life changes than those Naomi experienced. Those traumatic events in her life included moving to a foreign land, her husband's dying, her sons' getting married to women of a different faith and culture, her sons' dying, and one of her daughters-in-law's parting ways with her. Let's just summarize her situation by saying that the stress factors in Naomi's life were significant! Her close relationship with God, though, held the effects of stress at bay. That same kind of relationship with Him is still available to us today.

Ruth gives us good insights into the way Naomi handled not only the stresses, but also the times of transition in her life. In each case, she positioned herself mentally, physically, and emotionally in a way that her God would lift her to her next new normal. When we are in the midst of transition, we would be wise to do the same.

Transitions are the zones where we find ourselves between what was and what is yet to be. They are times when we must begin to establish a new normal. Transitions can be incredibly scary because the old has gone but the new has yet to come fully.

Not long before his death, Henri Nouwen wrote a book called *Sabbatical Journey*. In it he tells of some friends of his who were trapeze artists, called the

Flying Roudellas.

The Roudellas told Nouwen there's a special relationship between the flyer and the catcher on the trapeze. The flyer is the one who lets go, and the catcher is the one who catches. As the flyer swings high above the crowd on the trapeze, the moment comes when he must let go. He arcs out into the air. His job is to remain as still as possible and wait for the strong hands of the catcher to pluck him from the air.

One of the Flying Roudellas told Nouwen, "The flyer must never try to catch the catcher. The flyer must wait in absolute trust. The catcher will catch him, but he must wait."

What a perfect image of what it means to handle transition well. As we let go of what we've known, of what has been normal for us, we are in transition until we let God reach us for our next adventure. We can't fully grasp what is next on our own. We only figure that out when we are in His grip.

Through the years, we will experience transitions, and our daughters-in-law will notice how we move through them. We need to keep in mind that our transitions are windows of opportunity for us to alleviate some of the fears they, too, may face over the years as life requires them to make similar transitions. Holding in our minds the image of the trapeze artist transitioning and positioning, we can picture ourselves confidently waiting for God to catch us. Learning how to transition well is definitely one of those lessons that is caught, not taught.

Consider a daughter-in-law's point of view:

I understand that my mother-in-law is in transition, but sometimes I think she's more comfortable being in the transition phase than she thinks she'll be if she moves on to what God has prepared for her. I wonder how I can best encourage her to move into her new normal.

Be the mother-in-law you wish you had:

- Pray that when times of transition come, you will confidently reach toward God and let Him place you well for your new normal.
- Share with your daughter-in-law that your times of transition do not need to become worrisome for her. Let her know that God has a plan.
- Think of new ways you might be able to bless your daughter-in-law once you've passed through the transition and can interact with her

from your new normal.

- Remember how you are feeling as you transition so that you can recall those emotions of fear and uncertainty when your daughter-in-law is going through a time of transition. In other words, when your daughter-in-law is in the throws of a transition, remember what that feels like and give her a break.

"During the transition period there will be a large but never complete overlap between the problems that can be solved by the old and by the new paradigm."
—THOMAS S. KUHN

Build Your Life With the Future in Mind

"For I know the plans I have for you," says the Lord. "They are plans for good and not for disaster, to give you a future and a hope."
JEREMIAH 29:11 NLT

Every moment of today is connected to a moment of tomorrows. What we do today matters beyond today. When Naomi moved to Moab from her homeland of Judah, her actions built a foundation upon which her family would be built. Her sons would reach manhood, and each would look for a wife among a people whose culture and religion did not match her own. When she decided to leave Moab after her husband's death and encouraged her daughters-in-law to return to their Moabite families, her decision allowed the women to chart a course for the future of their own choosing. Considering these and other aspects of Naomi's biography gives us insight into the importance our present decisions, words, and actions have on our future relationships with our daughters-in-law.

The best way to approach the future is to envision what you hope it to be, and then invite, through your words and actions, those you care about toward that dream. If you want to have a daughter-in-law who trusts you, be dependable; if you want her to love your son well, encourage him to love

her well; if you want her to grow in her love for God, make sure you aren't faltering in your own walk of faith. There are so many ways you can set up the environment for her future success, but you are going to have to think about the specifics of what that looks like in the unique relationship you have with her.

I was praying for my sons' wives even while my sons were infants, so by the time I met the women they were going to marry, I was more than ready to know my "daughters"! I remember well the day I met each one.

I met Lisa when Josh brought her to our home to introduce her to us. Her childhood home was just a few blocks away, but she had attended private schools while Josh attended public ones, so their paths never crossed until that summer. Home from her music studies at college in Tennessee, she was working at the kids' summer day camp, where Josh also had taken a summer job—a respite from his pursuit of a business degree. It was early evening when Josh brought her to our door. He was beaming, and Lisa was beautiful—a strikingly fit petite, filled to the brim with joy. I took pictures that captured her gorgeous smile while she captured our hearts. Joel and I had a lighthearted conversation with them before they took off for dinner together. I love Lisa. She and I share a special bond, in part because she is my first and long-awaited "daughter." The incredible joy of our first meeting continues today and is a significant part of my dream for the future with my daughter-in-law Lisa.

Serendipitously, I met Rhonda before Isaac did. That was fun! My husband and I were at a restaurant having dinner with her parents. Her family had recently moved to Orlando from Phoenix and had begun attending Northland, A Church Distributed, where my husband serves as pastor. Rhonda was working on her degree in social work at a college in Winter Park, a suburb of Orlando. At her mom's request, she stopped by the restaurant to meet us on her way to an event. She was absolutely radiant, very classy, and extremely gifted socially. Joel and I commented to each other, after she left, that she was someone our son Isaac would love to meet. It wasn't long before Isaac did just that, as they were designated partners on a church outreach to take inner city kids to the beach. Four months later, they were engaged. When you know, you know. I love Rhonda. She and I have a special bond, in part because we share very similar lives—each of us is a pastor's wife. The idealness of our first meeting continues today, and it is a significant part of my dream for the future with my daughter-in-law Rhonda.

Last, but not least, I met the love of our youngest son's life, Elizabeth, aka Lizzy. Joel had been through college, medical school, and an internship before he found Lizzy, and she was definitely worth his wait. Her brother was attending Summit Church in Orlando, where Isaac serves as senior pastor, and that led to Joel and Lizzy's connecting through a social networking site. Because they were living in two different states at the time—Joel was in Virginia doing his internship as a physician, and Lizzy was in Florida singing with the Orlando Opera—it was months before they met each other face to face. But soon after they met, we got to meet her, too. The entire Hunter family gathered at a local restaurant and was introduced to this brilliant and beautiful woman. Her quick wit engaged us all. I love Lizzy. She and I have a special bond, in part because we teamed up for a year and together ministered to pastors' wives on behalf of the Global Pastors Wives Network. The family feel of our first meeting continues today, and it is a significant part of my dream for the future with my daughter-in-law Lizzy.

As I said previously, that first memorable get-together between a mother- and daughter-in-law doesn't have a script, but there is a bottom line: A son falls in love, and his mom gains a daughter. And that can be an awesome gain.

Consider a daughter-in-law's point of view:
Maybe my relationship with my mother-in-law will improve as the years go along. That would be great.

Be the mother-in-law you wish you had:
- Pray for insights into your daughter-in-law's world so that you really can be a blessing in her life.
- Determine what you should say and do by considering how your words and actions will impact the future.
- Encourage your daughter-in-law in her areas of strength; inspire her toward a future that uses her strengths.

> *"As for the future, your task is not to foresee it, but to enable it."*
> —ANTOINE DE SAINT-EXUPÉRY

Chapter Six

Prioritize Love and Patience

G OD, DELIVER US from mediocrity, give us a vision high, a pride low, a faith wide, a love deep, and patience long." I love this petition from Bob Moorehead's book *The Growth Factor*. His appeal to God is also an invitation for us to engage life and relationships on a whole new level.

Picture the difference in the world—no, wait, just picture the difference in families if every person would love deeply and be patient. In fact, just imagine what your family might be like if you were loving and patient. Astounding blessings come with such a godly approach to life.

Consider Timing

There's an opportune time to do things, a right time for everything on the earth.
ECCLESIASTES 3:1

Did you ever have a great idea—go to a lot of trouble to make your daughter-in-law's day, only to have her respond with a forced smile or a

distracted, "Thanks"? When we are hoping for high-fives all around, but the one we've "blessed" has an obvious lack of awareness concerning our thoughtful effort, it can be disconcerting. If we are greeted with such a lackluster response, consider the possibility that it isn't our idea or our effort that was lacking. Maybe we just overlooked the significance of good timing.

Here's an example: You decide you would like to drop off something for your daughter-in-law to surprise her, but inherent in surprise is the fact that she won't be expecting you. There is a very real possibility that when she sees you at the door, her stress level will partially blind her to your kindness.

There is an easy way to know whether or not you should just drop in on her whenever you'd like and stay as long as you feel like staying. If she has always insisted that you stop by anytime you feel like it and has begged you to stay as long as you can every time you do, then it's okay to drop by. Otherwise, give her a heads-up that you would like to come by, and ask her what would be a good time for you to arrive. In other words, set her up to succeed, not in meeting your expectations, but in meeting her own!

The purpose in letting her know ahead of time what your plans are is not to make sure she has certain things accomplished before you arrive. It's not about her house meeting your standard of perfection, or your grandchildren being freshly bathed, or the scent of baking cookies wafting through the house as you step over the threshold. To set up her success, you simply need to give her the opportunity to greet you in the way she would like. This seems like common sense, but I'm amazed at how many women assume their daughters-in-law just love for them to drop by unannounced—and even more amazed by how many women couldn't care less whether their daughters-in-law would love it or not.

If our desire is to be helpful or even just encouraging, we have to consider the timing of our assistance. Timing is a critical aspect of helpfulness. Let me give you a personal example. I enjoy having our grandchildren come to our house to play, but when my sons and daughters-in-law are going to be gone overnight, I love to stay with my grandchildren in their own homes; they sleep better in their own beds, and their routines are not interrupted. I'm very task-oriented, and I thoroughly enjoy doing anything to help out my daughters-in-law. The tricky part for me is to know what is most helpful to do in the time I'm there, and what they might interpret as meddling or overbearing.

I'm almost paranoid about this because it seems to me that people who are meddling and overbearing never believe themselves to be either. A friend of mine told me how her mother-in-law would come to their house to watch their kids for an afternoon and would rearrange the furniture in half the rooms in their house to "make better use of the space." It's an understatement to say that my friend didn't appreciate her efforts. Another friend said once when her mother-in-law stayed at her house to watch the children for a day, my friend arrived home to discover that there were no clothes in the closets. None. Her mother-in-law had gathered up all of them and took them to the drop-off laundry and dry cleaners because "it looked like they could use a good cleaning." To this day, my friend holds a grudge against her mother-in-law for her "helpfulness." Can you blame her? It's important, before we act, to ask ourselves, "Is this the right time to do this? Could she perceive what I'm about to do as embarrassing to her—an unspoken indictment on the way she cares for her family—rather than helpful?"

If we really want to bless our daughters-in-law, let's consider not only how we can help, but also when the perfect time for us to do so might be. And if we already have "helped" them in ways that they have perceived, rightly or wrongly, to be inappropriate or implicitly critical of them, we need to apologize! It's always a perfect time to do that!

Consider a daughter-in-law's point of view:
God, give me the courage to be upfront with my mother-in-law about what is and isn't helpful. And please don't let her feel rejected personally when I do choose to reject an offer of help.

Be the mother-in-law you wish you had:
- Pray for insights into not just how you can bless your daughter-in-law, but when you can.
- Be patient with her, always assume the best of her, and focus on her strengths.
- Check your motives, as well as your timing. Do you truly want to assist her in something she would like accomplished, or are you trying to improve her in some way? There is a big difference.

"Life is all about timing . . . the unreachable becomes reachable, the unavailable become available, the unattainable . . . attainable. Have the patience; wait it out. It's all about timing."
—STACEY CHARTER

Remain Flexible

If you had any idea what this Scripture meant—"I prefer a flexible heart to an inflexible ritual"—you wouldn't be nitpicking like this.
MATTHEW 12:7

All of us experience, on occasion, difficulties, delays, and frustrations when dealing with people. If we are going to be successful in our relationships, we have to know how to hold fast to our principles while being flexible in the ways we live them out. Flexing is a valuable attribute. It is the way we modify our methods to be effective in our goals.

Set her up to succeed, not in meeting your expectations, but in meeting her own!

Every mother-in-law has a perfectly valid reason to have a been-there-done-that attitude when she is interacting with her daughter-in-law. But if we mothers-in-law do have it, we are going to make it next to impossible for our daughters-in-law to enjoy being with us. It's easy to see why we may be tempted to engage with them from that I-know-more-than-you-know perspective. We, most likely, have been married longer than they have, we have raised our children, and we have trained for and pursued our callings inside and/or outside our homes. They are still in the early stages of all of that. If we come to them from an I-know-more-than-you-know perspective, our motivation is probably to get them to do what we did or get them to avoid doing what we did. The problem with that is, our daughters-in-law are adults—women, not little girls—and what they desire to learn from us they will find out by taking the initiative to ask or, more likely, by simply observing.

We are all different, so our reasons for making our daughters-in-law feel as though we know what's best for them vary greatly. Those of us who think our way is the only way, or even simply the best way, have diverse reasons for insisting our daughters-in-law do what we did. Some of us just love being a boss; others need to be needed. Some of us fear the choices they may make if they do life differently from the way we did; others need the personal validation that daughters-in-law who copy our ways bring.

If we are going to encourage our daughters-in-law in inspiring ways, we will focus more on righteous goals and be less exacting about the methods they choose to achieve them. There is a saying that nothing is set in stone. Ways that we have chosen to go about living a godly and rewarding life can be altered without doing any damage to our principles or goals. New ways to reach goals that will never change may be much better than old ways.

I'm reminded of the story about the young woman who picked up a ham at the grocery store and brought it home. Her husband took one look at it and asked her why she didn't have the butcher cut off the end of the ham.

"Why would you want the end cut off?" she asked.

He replied that his mother had always done it that way.

Since the husband's mother was visiting, they asked her why she always cut off the end of the ham. "That was the way my mother always did it," she replied.

Deciding to solve this three-generation mystery, the husband, his mother, and the wife decided to call the grandmother. Her response to their ham question, "Oh, I cut off the end of the ham because my roaster was too small to cook it in one piece."

As tempting as it is to cling to tried-and-true methods of accomplishing goals, the only things we really need to be clinging to are the goals themselves. Methods of reaching those goals—everything from how to cook the ham, to how to succeed in school, to how to be a great wife, to how to raise great children—vary from generation to generation. Ways of doing things do become outdated and ineffective, and we need to embrace new and different approaches that help our daughters-in-law accomplish the goals.

Being flexible, able to adapt to a world that is constantly changing, requires a good mind and a willingness to learn new things. When we do, we benefit! Take social networking, for example. How much do you miss out on your daughter-in-law's life because you don't know how to turn on a computer,

but she is on a social networking site such as Facebook, posting pictures and personal vignettes? Opening her diary wouldn't give you any better glimpse into her world than opening her "profile" and checking out her "wall." And the best part is, you are welcome to do so! Don't get intimidated by new ways of doing things. You can learn, and it is important to be a learner as well as a teacher. Often, simply choosing to be a lifelong learner can build better interactions with your daughter-in-law. Decades from now, when she is frustrated because the way she's always done things isn't working all that well anymore, she may recall your willingness to never stop learning new ways of doing things and be motivated to do the same.

Consider a daughter-in-law's point of view:

I actually like it when my mother-in-law asks me to help her figure out something she honestly has no clue about. I hate it when she asks and acts like she doesn't know how to do something, but really does.

Be the mother-in-law you wish you had:
- Pray that you will know when you need to be flexible and what principles you should hold to without wavering.
- Keep learning, and don't be afraid to implement new ways of reaching old goals.
- Know yourself. Are you being bossy, picky, wimpy, or otherwise unlovely in your relationship with your daughter-in-law? If so, quit that.

> *"Commit with unwavering tenacity to every godly goal, and to boundless flexibility in the ways you approach those goals."*
> —ANONYMOUS

Treasure the Positive

So they hurried off and found Mary and Joseph, and the baby, who was lying in the manger. When they had seen him, they spread the word concerning what had been told

them about this child, and all who heard it were amazed at what the shepherds said to them. But Mary treasured up all these things and pondered them in her heart.
Luke 2:16-19 NIV

"Why were you searching for me?" he asked. "Didn't you know I had to be in my Father's house?" But they did not understand what he was saying to them. Then he went down to Nazareth with them and was obedient to them. But his mother treasured all these things in her heart. And Jesus grew in wisdom and stature, and in favor with God and men.
Luke 2:49-54 NIV

If there is anything a mother treasures more than positive comments about her child, it might be the revelations that her child shares with her about himself. In the verses that you just read, we see Mary, a mom, treasuring what the shepherds had to say about her newborn son, Jesus. And twelve years later, Scripture highlights another time when she treasured words she was hearing, and this time, they were the words of Jesus Himself. When Jesus began to share His point of view and acknowledge that He was God's Son, she treasured His perspective.

What does Mary's treasuring of those comments have to do with you and your daughter-in-law? Lots.

From these verses in Luke, we learn two ways to grow close to the adult females who are now related to us. Listen to what others who have seen them and have come to love them have to say about them, and treasure those good perspectives. Then, listen to what these women, who fell in love with our sons, tell us about themselves. If we are good listeners, they may continue to share insights with us throughout the years as their role in our sons' lives matures over their lifetimes. As we treasure their viewpoints, they will know how much we love them.

Jesus told us, "Where your treasure is, there your heart will be also" (Matthew 6:21, NIV). Think about that. It is likely the opposite of what you have assumed to be true. When Jesus commented about our hearts, aka emotions, following our investments, He didn't define those investments as only financial ones. He was referencing a principle larger than that. He was letting us know that the way to feel connected, the way to care about something or someone, is to invest in that thing or person.

If we don't feel close to our daughters-in-law, if loving them eludes us,

Jesus says that by investing in them, we will come to love them. He states that our emotions will follow our investments. It is no oversight that He doesn't specify exactly what our investments should be. Those vary, because we must invest what is valuable to us!

There is a broad range of investments we can make in our daughters-in-law. Among the options: We can invest our time in prayer for them, our energy in helping them with things that meet their own good goals, and our material resources when we know doing so points them toward maturity and selflessness in God's calling on their lives.

We aren't going to grow closer to our sons' wives simply by trying to get ourselves to care about what they care about or by thinking we really should just try to like them better than we do. That is impossible. It is a backward, messed-up way of doing things. Jesus has let us know that the way we really begin to care and develop passion and excitement about them is to invest in them, and then we will see heartfelt feelings follow our investments. So, if we want to honestly care about our daughters-in-law, we have to take what is valuable to us—our prayers, our time, our energy, and our material resources—and pour those things into our daughters-in-law, no matter how we feel about them at the moment. With that, our love for them will grow beyond our best imagination.

Sometimes it is difficult to wrap our minds around the fact that we have adult females whom we didn't raise smack dab in the middle of "our" families. And they got there simply by borrowing ink pens and cosigning marriage contracts with our sons. It's amazing that it took contractions to get our sons, but only contracts to get our daughters-in-law—shouldn't words so similar have a lot more in common than those two do? It is great to get "daughters" without having to go through labor and delivery, though. Sometimes I treasure my daughters-in-law for that reason alone!

Consider a daughter-in-law's point of view:
It is so much easier to be my best when my mother-in-law is thinking the best of me.

Be the mother-in-law you wish you had:
- Pray that you will invest wisely in your daughter-in-law.
- Give both tangible and intangible gifts to her.
- Focus on and encourage her with everything good you hear about her, and commit to prayer anything not so good.

"Often the only way to find a treasure is to keep moving through the dark until you stumble over it."
—ANONYMOUS

Chapter Seven

Value Your Son's Wife

THE RELATIONSHIP BETWEEN our daughters-in-law and us will be strained if we assign our married sons roles that they were not meant to have in our lives. If we picture these married men as our little boys, or if we look to them for support and encouragement that would be better sought in our spouses, or if we idolize them, believing they're perfect, we will make our daughters-in-law's lives more difficult.

There are behaviors that wives tend to practice when "moms" treat their married sons like children or consider them their sole sources of support and encouragement. Our interactions with our sons do affect their wives' interactions with them.

See Your Boys as Men

When I was a child, I talked like a child, I thought like a child, I reasoned like a child; now that I have become a man, I am done with childish ways and have put them aside.

1 CORINTHIANS 13:11 AMP

We might all wholeheartedly agree with this familiar verse of Scripture, but what's a mom to do if she sees her married son retain childish ways? Many a mom made an assumption long ago that the old saying "Boys will be boys" is true. During sons' growing-up years, it certainly seems to be true, especially for a decade or so when the little guys are alternating between antics that are crazy and ones that are gross. But if we tell ourselves that male children are supposed to be rambunctious, loud, and generally immature, we may start to believe that is part of their charm.

But now, even if we are still choosing to look at these grown men through a "mom" lens that distorts their current age to ten, it's difficult to justify any lingering immaturity. In hindsight, we realize that "Boys will be boys" is not the adage we should have been embracing. The truth is, "Boys will be men." If that was our understanding as we raised our sons, we probably find it relatively easy to enjoy them now as mature adults: husbands with wives, and fathers with children. Not only do sons raised by parents who value that principle seem to be mature; they likely are mature. Maturity is a blessing that comes from "training up a child in the way he should go," rather than training him up in the way he should stay. But if we chose the way-he-should-stay approach and cherished our sons' immaturity, either because we didn't know it would matter, or because we didn't care what the results of that would be, there is a pretty high probability that today our very big boys still act like they need mothering. And their wives are not going to be happy about that.

When "Boys will be boys" was and continues to be a mother's preferred view of a married son, interactions between them are distorted. And that "He's still my boy" attitude creates unnecessary issues for our daughters-in-law. The way we interact with our sons does affect our daughters-in-law's interactions both with us and with their husbands.

It's never too late for moms to choose to see their sons as adults, as men fully capable of handling their own lives and caring for their families. When we voice our confidence in our sons—act toward them in ways that show we trust them to capably handle whatever comes their way, and when we treat our sons as we would any adult, we do our daughters-in-law a great favor.

Consider a daughter-in-law's point of view:

I don't know how to respond to my mother-in-law's apparent inability to see her son as a mature adult. I'm praying her view of him doesn't impact the way

he sees himself or, worse yet, the way I see him.

Be the mother-in-law you wish you had:
- Pray that your son will turn to the Lord to help him achieve everything he is capable of being.
- Honor your daughter-in-law by choosing to honor and respect her husband.
- Cherish the memories of your son's boyhood, applaud his present, and pray for his future as a godly husband and father.

> *"It kills you to see them grow up. But I guess it would kill*
> *you quicker if they didn't."*
> —BARBARA KINGSOLVER

Interact With Your Daughter-in-law's Husband

So a man will leave his father and mother and be united with his wife.
GENESIS 2:24 NCV

We all know women who'd rather be friends with than parents to their children, but "peer-enting" isn't parenting. There are several reasons why some moms fall into it anyway. Single moms and moms whose husbands are distant geographically or emotionally are especially susceptible to adopting such a noninstructive role. Any mom, though, can fall into this misguided approach to parenting. Ironically, those who choose to interact with their young sons as though they are their friends will find it difficult to have relationships with their married sons that aren't built on the moms' needs. Many moms who choose to peer-ent rather than parent will try to maintain their close relationship with their married sons through a litany of their needs.

Few things have more potential to frustrate daughters-in-law than the expectations mothers-in-law have of the daughters-in-law's husbands. Women who hold unreasonable expectations of married sons (unreasonable in volume

and/or scope) often are oblivious to the fact that their plans for their sons' lives are burdening their daughters-in-law even more than they are burdening their sons. Presuming on their sons' closeness and support feels so normal to these moms that they would be shocked if someone were to point out that they are expecting too much. And heaven forbid, the daughters-in-law are the ones to point that out!

So how can we determine if our expectations of our sons are unreasonable? Assuming they are would be a better baseline for analyzing that than assuming they aren't.

If we take time to think through the challenges and obligations they have as husbands and fathers, we will be less likely to use copies of our to-do lists to stay connected with them. Personal to-do lists are always going to be a part of our lives, and as we age, it only gets easier to ask them to handle things than to figure out other ways to get them done. But we didn't raise sons to have someone whose purpose in life was to come to our aid. We raised them to be godly men who could be effective in making the world a better place through their own work and families. If that wasn't our prayer from the beginning of their lives, we can make that our prayer for them from now on.

It's not that we can never ask anything of our sons or their wives, but we need to steer clear of a lifestyle of imposition. If we give our married sons and their wives opportunities to set the parameters for their relationship with us, we will find much greater joy than we could ever find in their meeting our demands.

Consider a daughter-in-law's point of view:

My husband feels so responsible for his mom. The guilt he feels when he "fails" to meet her expectations and the frustration he feels when he doesn't have time to try to meet them weigh heavily on me and the kids.

Be the mother-in-law you wish you had:

- Pray that you will become aware of any expectations or burdens you place on your son.
- Acknowledge the honor it is to you when your son prioritizes his wife and his children.
- Ask yourself, before you impose on your son for assistance or encouragement, "Is there someone else who could help me with this?"

- When your son has spent his time, energy, and resources helping you out, don't thank him only; also thank his wife for "sharing" her husband. If he was away from her for a significant time to accomplish something for you, acknowledge that you know the investment he made in your day had an impact on hers; send her flowers, along with your word of thanks.

> *"We don't raise heroes, we raise sons; but if we treat them like sons should be treated, they'll turn out to be heroes."*
> —ANONYMOUS

Resist the Temptation to Worship Your Son

You must not have any other god but me.
EXODUS 20:3 NLT

"Can I name my son God?" That question was submitted to an online Q&A. The response: "No, but Jesus might be a good alternative." Interesting. Neither the question, nor its answer had crossed my mind before, but when I read the exchange, it made me start thinking about some of the moms I know who give their sons top priority in their lives. Once again, the temptation toward this may be greater for the mom who is single or is distant from her husband, but no mom is exempt.

At least some credit is due to the online inquirer, who had the wherewithal to ask if it was okay to assign her son a moniker that she felt would suit him. Some of us actually treat our sons as gods, but won't admit to ourselves that is what we are doing, and even fewer of us who treat them that way have ever considered naming our sons God. Others may notice how high the pedestals are that we've placed our sons on, but they aren't likely to mention to us that we have lost perspective. And they shouldn't have to; if we love our sons more than anyone or anything, if they are our greatest delight, or we depend on them more than we depend on God, it should cross our minds that we have given them the status of a god. And we've set up their wives for a rough time

because being married to a god isn't easy.

If we catch ourselves always taking our sons' side, seeing no possible way anything could ever be their fault or due to their failure, if we feel that they can do no wrong, we might better be described as their worshipers than as their moms. The mother of Jesus, Mary, was the only woman the world has ever known who could have rightfully looked to her son as God. But she didn't make a habit of doing that because she had a specific role in his life. A mom's assignment in the early years is always to help her son grow "in wisdom and in stature and in favor with God and all the people" (Luke 2:52, NLT). We can't worship our sons and at the same time help them mature. We've got to choose between those two ways of interacting with them. If we focus our worship on God and value our sons' maturity, our sons, and their wives, will be blessed in the long term.

Our daughters-in-law deserve a spouse who loves the Lord, is wise and strong, and gets along with people. To the best of our abilities, we hopefully saw to it that while our sons were young, they developed in those realms. If instead we treated our sons like gods, serving them, catering to their whims, and praising them for their existence alone, then ironically, we could only offer our daughters-in-law immature men who will run away from them the moment maturity is required in the marriage. If that's what we did, we can't go back and change it, but we can acknowledge that in doing so, we did neither our sons, nor their wives any favors. And going forward, we can be wiser about how we express our love for them. The wisdom to do that well will be found in the overflow of love we have when we prioritize our relationship with the real God.

Last winter, I was on a plane, seated beside a woman about my age. The flight took only one hour, but the vast amount of information that she was able to unload about her family in just sixty minutes was astounding. I never even learned her name because there wasn't a break in her monologue that was long enough to ask it, and she never asked me anything. In an avalanche of words, she drifted to commenting on her "amazing youngest son, who married a wonderful girl three years ago and then suddenly, just a month ago, left her right after their first child was born with disabilities." My seatmate was bewildered by her "incredible son's behavior." She kept stressing to me that she and her husband had given this very talented young man everything his heart desired. Money had never been an issue because they had been blessed in business, and they knew God would want them to "shower him in blessings,"

which they did.

This woman was a son worshiper, and through this sad turn of events, she was just beginning to realize it. Buried in a situation that she inadvertently and almost singlehandedly had created, she was trying to explain herself and him to a total stranger. "He's a good boy. He probably just needed some space. He's an artist, you know, and artists, really great artists, need their space."

As the plane was landing, she grabbed my arm and said, "I'm going to bring my daughter-in-law and grandson into our home for now. She doesn't want to come, but I'll make it happen, and I think my son will be back one day."

What was there to say to her? It didn't matter that I didn't know, because she literally stopped talking only after she had grabbed her carry-on bag and headed for the exit. Knowing that God always has His reasons for bringing people into our lives, I am wondering if He brought this woman into mine just for you. Is your life centered on your son?

A strong relationship with God is the only cure for our "other god" issues. Developing that relationship with Him takes time and effort. But having no other gods besides God means giving Him priority over our relationships with everyone and everything—sons and daughters-in-law included.

Consider a daughter-in-law's point of view:
I wish my mother-in-law would center her life on something besides my husband.

Be the mother-in-law you wish you had:
- Pray that your son will be a mature partner in his marriage relationship.
- Pray that your daughter-in-law will have the grace and wisdom to love her husband toward ever-increasing maturity, and know that your season of opportunity to help him mature has ended.
- Worship only God.

"There is an enduring tenderness in the love of a mother to a son
that could easily transcend all other affections of the heart—she must assure
it does not transcend her affection for God or her spouse."
—WASHINGTON IRVING

Chapter Eight

Tackle Insecurities

WHILE IT'S TRUE that "mom" is a term with no term limits, as a boy changes from a child to a man, and becomes a husband and eventually a father, his mom's responsibilities change radically. And change is always a petri dish for insecurities; they flourish in times of change.

The mother-in-law/daughter-in-law relationship is a complicated human connection. It comes with inherent mismatched perspectives—two radically different views of the same man. One woman always will see him first as a man, her protector; the other always will see him first as her boy, someone she needs to protect. Understanding that your daughter-in-law has this perspective different from your own is critical. If you don't understand that or simply refuse to acknowledge it, your relationship can be plagued by insecurities—overbearing demands, despairing thoughts, and crazy fears. Never underestimate anyone's insecurities, not even your own.

Drop Demands

I am not commanding you, but I want to test the sincerity of your love by comparing it with the earnestness of others.
2 CORINTHIANS 8:8 NIV

In Greek mythology, Venus, the goddess of love and beauty, was Psyche's mother-in-law. While I'm tempted to comment here about a daughter-in-law actually being named Psyche, I won't. Back to the story: Venus decreed she would not accept Psyche as a daughter-in-law unless she performed several preposterous tasks. In fact, Venus generated trouble for Psyche even before Venus became Psyche's mother-in-law. The reason: As beautiful as Venus was, everyone was ignoring her and paying attention to Psyche.

Livid with jealousy, Venus sent her son, Cupid, with his famous arrows to make Psyche fall in love with an ugly, grotesque creature. But when Cupid saw her, he was so startled by Psyche's beauty that he accidentally scratched himself with his own arrow. That caused him to fall madly, hopelessly in love with Psyche, and he chose to secretly marry her. But he did so on the condition that she must never look at him. Each day, before each sunrise, he would leave a lonely and increasingly curious Psyche.

One night curiosity got the best of Psyche, so she lit the lamp and looked at her sleeping husband. It was love at first sight for her and rapid flight for Cupid, who was crushed at this betrayal of his trust. Psyche then roamed the earth in search of her husband. Venus, her mother-in-law, now aware of her marriage to Cupid, put Psyche through many trials in attempts to prove her worthy of Venus's darling son. Psyche managed to meet most of these trials with success.

Eventually, Psyche failed one of Venus's tests, and that failure caused her to fall into a coma. In spite of that, before too long, Cupid managed to find her. Psyche was awakened, and the reunited couple joined Zeus and a slightly grudging Venus on Mount Olympus, where they all lived "happily ever after."

The stereotyping of mothers-in-law as demanding women is not new. That Greek myth has been passed down for thousands of years through myriad generations. In every generation, mothers-in-law need to avoid the temptation to make

demands of adult sons and their wives. Whether you have a daughter-in-law who would strive to meet your demands or one who would disregard them altogether, demands are inappropriate. We need to ask ourselves if we are weighing down our sons' wives with activities and responsibilities that we would find frustrating to accomplish if our mothers-in-law were demanding them of us.

If your daughter-in-law has "failed your tests"—if she doesn't keep house to your standards, land the job you wanted her to have, discipline her children as you deem appropriate, and so on—and now you find her to be nonresponsive toward you, it's time to take the perspective offered from the mountaintop, and maybe one of these days, she, like Psyche, will join you in a higher level of perspective.

Consider a daughter-in-law's point of view:

If I try to meet my mother-in-law's demands, she likely will see me forever in the role of a child or her servant. But if I fail to meet them, will there be any relationship at all?

Be the mother-in-law you wish you had:

* Be aware of your personal insecurities, and don't take action based on them.
* Phrase your requests of your daughter-in-law in the form of invitations.
* Take note of her responses in your interactions with her. If she is nonresponsive or frustrated, she may be interpreting your communication as demanding. If so, communicate differently.
* Give her time to be the initiator. You may be pleasantly surprised at what she invites you to if you never pressure her.
* Pray that you will never intentionally or unintentionally set up your daughter-in-law to fail.

"Love is the ability and willingness to allow those that you care for to be what they choose for themselves without any insistence that they satisfy you."
—WAYNE DYER

Don't Despair

We've been surrounded and battered by troubles, but we're not demoralized; we're not sure what to do, but we know that God knows what to do; we've been spiritually terrorized, but God hasn't left our side; we've been thrown down, but we haven't broken.
2 Corinthians 4:8-9

Despair is not an option—at least for those of us who are Christians. Why? Because despair diminishes our ability to love well. While mother-in-law/daughter-in-law stereotypes tend to play up untenable situations and give the impression "that's just how it is; there is nothing we can do about it," that's almost never true. We can do something. We can determine our actions, reactions, and whether we will unleash or restrain our feelings.

There are practical steps we can take when the relationship challenges cause us to move from being modestly frustrated to overwhelmingly sad. First, we can determine if part of our dismay is due to the fact that we have tucked into the backs of our minds a script of the dream we imagined for our sons and their wives, and are appalled that they are not following that script. We need to remember that not only did they never get a copy of it, but we were not meant to write or direct the script of their lives together! They get to write and direct their own script.

Second, walls that exist between us, made up of cultural, religious, emotional, or personality differences, need not be permanent. Such things are huge challenges, but they are not insurmountable. All these things, though, pale in comparison to the angst we feel when we believe our daughters-in-law are demeaning or hurting our sons. The most important thing we can do to get past these or any other issues we have with them is to know what we can't do. We can't change them, and we can't rescue our sons.

We can ask God to redeem their situation and change us. If we are willing to throw away our scripts for their marriage and encourage them in any positive aspects of the life they are choosing to live, then our tendency toward despair will lessen. When we learn more about where our daughter-in-law is "coming from" and why she thinks the way she does, we chip away at the wall that has been built between us. And if we believe our son is hurting, we need

to remember that he is a man capable of holding his own—and there is always the remote possibility that we have misinterpreted their situation entirely and they both like the way their lives are going.

While we are praying for (not about) our daughters-in-law, we can take inventory of ways we might be contributing to building walls instead of bonds. Maybe they believe we are interfering, or being presumptuous or callous. They do have a right to be wrong about us, and their opinions count. So let's acknowledge our part in purposely or unwittingly helping to build any barriers that exist between us. As difficult as it is to look at adjusting how we think and act, it is one of the best things we can do to put cracks in the walls between us. The potential of a good relationship with our daughter-in-law always exists.

With the two or more decades of maturity that living longer than they have provides us, it's good for us to be the first to offer apologies and ask for forgiveness for our part in building walls. And this has to be done without requiring a response, let alone a preferred response, from them. We can do this. We are mature.

Consider a daughter-in-law's point of view:

Why would my mother-in-law even want a relationship with me? All I do is break her heart, frustrate her plans, and give myself more ways to fail if I do engage with her. I would like for us to have a good relationship, but I'm not sure I have the energy that relationship seems to require.

Be the mother-in-law you wish you had:

- Don't overreact to your daughter-in-law's words or actions.
- Give her "space." Sometimes being overly attentive, especially if it is perceived as nosiness or correction, will put Newton's third law of motion into play: "For every action there is an equal and opposite reaction."
- Use this difficult season of your relationship to spend time praying for her (not about her, but for her). Ask God to soften her heart and to give you His wisdom and peace.
- Lighten up. Go on with your life in ways that don't require the relationship with your daughter-in-law to be a pivotal point in your every day.

> *"Never despair, but if you must, then work on in despair."*
> —EDMUND BURKE

Fend Off Fear

Give your entire attention to what God is doing right now, and don't get worked up about what may or may not happen tomorrow. God will help you deal with whatever hard things come up when the time comes.
MATTHEW 6:34

Fear is always based on an impending scenario—what we think might happen or could come to pass. Fear is worry on steroids. When we are anxious, concerned, or downright fearful, we have moved our thoughts into an imaginary world where we speculate on various scenarios and leave reality behind. Fear blocks our ability to bless those around us. Worry sidelines the confidence we have in Christ because when we worry, we've gone to a place that doesn't exist and have tried to address circumstances that may never materialize.

Nancy Curtis, a pastor's wife from my hometown, said, "The reason we never should worry, Becky, is because our God is a real God. He helps us in our real needs. When we worry, create an imaginary situation in our minds, a fake place, our real God doesn't go into our pretend scenarios with us. When we worry, we go alone."

Now that is scary.

> Our real God doesn't go into our pretend scenarios with us. When we worry, we go alone.

Fears common to a mother-in-law are of two sorts: a fear of being left out or overlooked, and a fear of the future her son and her daughter-in-law face. These fears often are intertwined.

I know a sweet lady who raised a great son. He married an incredible woman when he was in his mid-twenties, after completing college and getting a good job. So far, so good. But as he and his wife move up the ladder of success, his mom constantly tries to get information about the details of their everyday lives. She just can't seem to stop herself. She was concerned enough about annoying them, though, that she brought it up to me over a cup of coffee. When I asked her why she couldn't give them a little more space, she responded, "If I don't know what is going on, I can only assume the worst."

"Worst?" I asked, trying to understand her concern.

"Yes, worst." Then she gave me a list of calamities and disasters that would freak out even professional "first responders."

"Why do you fear so much for them?" I asked. "They are two of the most competent, godly people I know. And God so obviously has His hand on them."

"Because if something happens that I could have warned them about and somehow prevented, I would never forgive myself. So, I worry for them because I feel like this is kind of my job, my role in their lives."

This woman was worried even when history and the current scenario for her son and his wife were great. Other moms worry for their struggling sons and daughters-in-law because "they've had nothing but troubles since the day they married." At least that is their perspective—though it may or may not be how their daughters-in-law and sons perceive their own situations. But the larger point is this: Whether the past was rosy or difficult, whether the present is going well or is a struggle, our fears can grow unchecked in the fantasy of yet unknowns.

Maybe you're a worrier, too. Maybe it's familiar fears themselves that make you feel like you are still a caring parent. The intense emotions that familiar fears generate may somehow make you feel you are a vital part of your son and daughter-in-law's present and a participant in their future. But I challenge you to leave a "worry world" that exists nowhere other than in your own mind, and instead regard their future only in your prayers. Your prayers can make a productive and positive difference in their life together. Your worry cannot. Your prayers will bless them now and in the future.

Consider a daughter-in-law's point of view:

Why does my mother-in-law worry? Nothing I say makes her stop fretting about our lives. Maybe I should share less? Maybe I should share more? Her fearfulness stresses me out more than our lives do!

Be the mother-in-law you wish you had:

* Think about this verse as you pray for yourself as well as for your son and his wife: "For God did not give us a spirit of timidity (of cowardice, of craven and cringing and fawning fear), but [He has given us a spirit] of power and of love and of calm and well-balanced mind and discipline and

self-control" (2 Timothy 1:7, AMP).

- Practice courage. Eleanor Roosevelt said this about courage: "Do the things you think you cannot do." Take a class, read a book, learn a skill, take a trip, volunteer ..., and bless your family with an upgraded you!
- If you want to worry less, live in the current time zone. Don't spend your days longing for the past or referencing an imaginary future. Those two time zones are real and connected only in the moment you're experiencing right now. Do now right.
- Tell your daughter-in-law that you are praying for her and are anticipating a wonderful future for her and your son. Then make sure you do pray!

"Worry gives even the smallest thing a big shadow."
—SWEDISH PROVERB

Chapter Nine

Keep the Big Picture in Mind

M Y HUSBAND ALWAYS talks about viewing life from the 30,000-foot level. Maybe that perspective naturally resonates with you, too. If so, you are blessed indeed. From that perspective, there is very little to trip you up, petty annoyances are few, and even a mountain can look like a molehill.

In fact, there is an old saying, "Live above the fly line." It was a recommendation of those living in the mountains who observed that there is an elevation above which flies do not thrive. Recognizing this fact, settlers put down roots at those elevations that did not require them to deal with such pesky annoyances. Emotionally, we all need to live above the "fly line." The vantage point from there allows us to more easily overlook the things that might otherwise drive us to distraction.

For the sake of inspiring both this generation and future ones, let's position ourselves in places where we can keep the big picture in mind.

Seek to Have God's Perspective

So if you're serious about living this new resurrection life with Christ, act like it.
Pursue the things over which Christ presides. Don't shuffle along, eyes to the ground,
absorbed with the things right in front of you. Look up, and be alert to what is going on
around Christ—that's where the action is. See things from his perspective.
COLOSSIANS 3:1-2

Perspectives vary, but it's been said, "If you never look up, you will believe you are at the highest point!" If we aren't intentional, we will view the world from the universal default perspective held by every human being: I am at the pinnacle of the universe, and from this vantage point, I have all the clarity I need. We all suffer this default—when we are shown a picture of a large group of people, we scan the faces searching for our own; when we think about what should be done in a certain circumstance, we reflect on the ways each decision might ultimately affect us personally; when we describe our interactions with others, we focus on how they made us feel. We all are self-centric unless we choose to consider situations and circumstances from the perspective of others. Considering another's perspective is not natural or easy to do, but it's critical to building healthy relationships.

The key perspective we should seek to have is God's perspective. Of course, we can't know everything He knows or see all that He sees, but "sometimes our humble hearts can help us more than our proud minds. We never really know enough until we recognize that God alone knows it all" (1 Corinthians 8:2-3). Simply acknowledging that we don't know everything and that there is only One who does is a God-given perspective. We learn in the book of Romans that we don't come to His perspective through only our own efforts, but by His desire to transform us from our simply copying the behaviors and customs of this world, to our letting Him transform us into new persons by changing the way we think. When we see our daughters-in-law from God's perspective, we will be likely to interact with them in the most beneficial ways.

To help me move toward God's perspective and see my sons' wives from a godly frame of reference, before I make pronouncements or begin to argue a point, I ask myself questions. I might ask, "Would I be glad for my grandchil-

dren to know someday that I said this to their mom?" Or I remind myself that God is a forever God, and ask, "How big of an issue is this in the entire scheme of things?" Sometimes I even ask myself, "Would I be glad I said this to her if (heaven forbid) she were to die tomorrow?" And one of my favorite ways to deal with any issue is to try to think through what Jesus might do faced with the same situation.

In fact, if we simply try to put ourselves in our daughters-in-law's shoes and see things from their perspectives, but fail to interpret their stances from a godly perspective, we are likely to assign wrong, or even evil, motives to them. Without a godly point of view, our take on their perspectives will only pit our impressions against theirs. That will result in a zero sum game. So rather than facing off, we have to face up to the greater reality and ask, "What is God's impression?"

Our relationships with these precious women ultimately aren't about them or us. Like every relationship we have, the greater significance of our relationships with them lies in God's Kingdom purposes. So the more we desire what God desires, the more significant the impact of every relationship we have.

Let me give you a practical example: If I want to cheer on my grandchildren in their activities, but then end up annoying my daughters-in-law with my need to know what, when, and where, the greater point of building good relationships can be put at risk. A good solution to things like this is most likely to be found when we are willing to simply ask: "Are there ways for me to get this information without bugging you? I hate adding another responsibility to your already full plate." Regrettably, all too often, while such unemotional, straightforward interaction is effective, it is the last thing to cross our minds.

As mothers-in-law, we have a responsibility to be mature. That mature perspective is demonstrated in our relationships with our daughters-in-law in a number of ways. Our feelings are not easily hurt, we accept responsibility for what we say and do, we don't give ultimatums, we don't have to "win," and we truly try to understand her perspective. In summary, we embrace the golden rule with our daughters-in law, and we do unto her as we hope (but do not require) that she would do unto us.

Consider a daughter-in-law's point of view:
I would appreciate a few more "How are you?" interactions and fewer "Here's how I am" interactions with my mother-in-law.

Be the mother-in-law you wish you had:

- Pray for a Christlike perspective.
- Picture yourself in your daughter-in-law's "shoes," and think through what situations might look like from her vantage point.
- Strive for maturity in every interaction with her.

> *"Mother-in-law and daughter-in-law are on the same team—*
> *just playing different positions."*
> —SANDY GRAVES

Bless the Generations

Understand, therefore, that the Lord your God is indeed God. He is the faithful God who keeps his covenant for a thousand generations and lavishes his unfailing love on those who love him and obey his commands.
DEUTERONOMY 7:9 NLT

Can our daughters-in-law stand on our shoulders? Literally, they can't, of course, but figuratively, they can. If we are strong emotionally and spiritually, we can offer them a vantage point they might not otherwise have. If we resolutely hold to the biblical foundations, our steady faith will help them feel secure. Every generation can go further than the preceding generation if it stands on the shoulders of that previous generation. Our daughters-in-law should have greater opportunities because of the faithful way we live our lives.

Some women had mothers-in-law who made their lives easier, others experienced quite the opposite of that blessing, and others, including me, never met the mothers of the men they married. But no matter what our foundational scenario, we are the generation through which blessings can begin or continue.

One way we bless the next generation is by assessing what we possess both spiritually and materially, then praying that we can have real wisdom in dis-

tinguishing which of those resources can benefit our daughters-in-law and which ones ultimately would be hindrances to them. How can resources possibly be hindrances? I have the perfect example: I know a woman whose son and daughter-in-law dedicated their lives to lifelong missionary work. Years ago, when they wouldn't take settings of china that had been in the woman's family for generations with them to Africa, she was crushed, and to this day, she remains irritated. This is what she told me a couple of years after the fact, "I tried to give her [my daughter-in-law] the most valuable, cherished thing I own, and she outright rejected it. She broke my heart." I ask myself, How is it that this woman can't see this from her daughter-in-law's viewpoint? But then I wonder, Could it be that I am sometimes this blind to the perspectives of the women my sons have married? That's a scary thought. I pray that my perspective will never be so limited.

Generally, we need to put less emphasis on trying to give our daughters-in-law clarity on what to do and how to do it, and more emphasis on personally living a godly life and being available for input upon request.

I never met my mother-in-law, but I love her with all my heart for bringing into this world and raising the man I married. She passed away just days before Joel's ordination into ministry and a few weeks before our first date. I never experienced her personal input; we had no good interactions and no bad ones. In her absence, I discovered the times a mother-in-law is greatly missed.

Here's when I missed her. I missed her when I married her son, and I couldn't tell her how much I love him and assure her I would cherish him for the rest of our lives. I missed her every time we made her a grandmother and six times over when her grandchildren made her a great grandmother. I still miss her every time my husband accomplishes something outstanding—goals that I know he would love for her to have seen him reach. And I miss not knowing my husband through her perspective . . . hearing her tell stories of his birth and childhood years. The bottom line is this: I significantly missed her at very specific times and for very specific reasons. Nearly all of my longing for a connection with her has been my desire to share good news with her and express gratitude for raising such a great son. I can't remember ever thinking, I wish my mother-in-law would tell me what to do right now, or, I would love to know what my mother-in-law thinks about this.

That little insight helped me decide what kind of mother-in-law I want to be. Over the years, I have heard so many women talk about how their mothers-

in-law lecture them on the way they should treat their husbands or raise their children. Some of them have been made to feel like they aren't good enough or aren't capable enough to be great wives or moms. I have never heard a word about what I ought or had to do. I want to be a mother-in-law who puts no more pressure or demands on my daughters-in-law than my mother-in-law has held me to from Heaven. I do want to be a mother-in-law who blesses the women my sons have married.

What is your heart's desire? Is your desire to be a blessing greater than your need to be blessed? Your answer to that question will set the tone for generations to come.

Consider a daughter-in-law's point of view:
There are some times I would actually miss my mother-in-law if she were not here.

Be the mother-in-law you wish you had:
- Pray for the generations yet to be born to your family.
- Be sure that what you want your daughter-in-law to have from you is what she wants to receive from you.
- Carry the countenance you hope she will one day model for her daughters-in-law.
- Write your mother-in-law a letter thanking her for some specific things she has done for you that you have appreciated.

"Each generation imagines itself to be more clever than the one that went before it, and wiser than the one that comes after it, but only the generation that is grateful to the previous one and encourages the next is truly clever or wise."
—PHILIP CROSBY

Inspire Your Daughter-in-Law

If all we get out of Christ is a little inspiration for a few short years, we're a pretty sorry lot.
1 CORINTHIANS 15:19B

In many ways, family is like a team. Each individual on a team must work independently, striving toward his or her personal best in order to effectively handle the role he or she has been given. When each one takes personal responsibility seriously, the family becomes a very strong team. When team members inspire one another toward the goals each has set individually, a very important goal for the group is met. Potential effectiveness of every person on that team is maximized when that happens. And so it is with families. When a mom is inspired, she becomes effective in her role, and makes it easier for her husband to be inspired and become effective in his. When children get inspired and become effective in their roles, their parents are able to have a greater impact for good in their communities and beyond. Family members impact one another along the way. That's a fact.

As families mature, how we adapt to the changing requirements of our mom role is important. We can rein in or release an atmosphere of inspiration and effectiveness. As daughters-in-law expand our ranks, one of the most effective ways we can continue to bless our families is, as it says in Philippians, to keep our eyes on the goal because God is always calling us onward—to Jesus. Keep running toward Him, and never turn back. I know from personal experience that no matter how long we have been running in His direction, there are challenges in continuing that journey. But if we hope to live this season of life well and finish strong, then getting ever closer to Christ must be our choice. If it is, our example may inspire others to persevere, to serve, and to sacrifice within their spheres of influence. Every family needs inspiring people.

One of the best examples of such a person is my sister-in-law, Michele. My husband has one sibling, a slightly older sister, who he claims made his childhood impossible because she was "perfect." Many teachers he had from first grade through his senior year would ask, "Why can't you be more like Michele?"

When I met Michele, she was already married and had a two-year-old exceptionally gifted son. Joel and I were engaged when she gave birth to a daughter, Janell. Arriving in this world months before she was due took its toll on Janell, permanently limiting her abilities to those of a typical preschool-age child. You can imagine the prayers we all prayed and the efforts that were made to change the realities of that situation. Through it all, and to this day, Michele inspired all of us with her faithful dedication to her God and her girl.

None of us can ever know the depths of her anguish or breadth of her fears as she faced the challenges that come with raising a special needs child, but we could all see how she chose to handle it.

Michele raised her gifted son and her special daughter and laid a foundation for each that maximized their gifts. Her son eventually married, and Sandy became part of the family.

No one could ever have imagined that nearly thirty years after Janell's birth, Michele's experience with Janell would make for a very special connection to her daughter-in-law. Incredibly, Sandy also gave birth to a gifted son, and only thirteen months later, gave birth to a premature daughter when her second pregnancy required an emergency C-section. The family flashed back, but Michele flashed forward, encouraging Sandy and standing resolute in prayer for her tiny new granddaughter. Michele must have been haunted by the irony of this situation in ways the rest of us could never fathom. But her history allowed her to embrace the early arrival of her granddaughter with a unique understanding of and sensitivity to her daughter-in-law's situation. She inspired Sandy, and everyone involved, with her encouraging words and through her ever-faithful modeling of a godly life. She spoke reminders of medical advancements that three decades surely had brought and requested as much prayer for Sandy as for her tiny granddaughter.

As it turns out, God, through the faithful prayers of hundreds of people and three decades of medical advancements, did provide an incredible outcome for Sandy's daughter. This beautiful girl was not affected in any way by her early arrival, and Michele and Sandy share a mother-in-law/daughter-in-law bond that is deep and precious.

We never know when God will use us to be an inspiration in a daughter-in-law's life, but we need to live like today could be that day. While we might never have a bonding situation that is as dramatic as Michele and Sandy's, we each will have moments, or perhaps even seasons, when how we handle what comes our way will impact our daughters-in-law. We may not know this side of heaven how our lives have impacted theirs. We can know, though, whether we are living our lives in ways that could inspire them along the way.

Consider a daughter-in-law's point of view:

When my mother-in-law knows I could use her help but ignores my need, or when she realizes there are times when she could encourage me but says noth-

ing, or when she could make a godly choice but gives in to temptation, does she think I don't notice or care? Well, I do.

Be the mother-in-law you wish you had:
- Pray for the inspiration Christ can give.
- Live in such a way that your life inspires your family toward spiritual maturity.
- Determine to finish strong. "Press on ... toward Jesus."
- Live in a way that makes God smile.

"Our deepest fear is not that we are inadequate. Our deepest fear is that we are powerful beyond measure. It is our light, not our darkness that most frightens us. We ask ourselves, 'Who am I to be brilliant, gorgeous, talented, fabulous?' Actually, who are you not to be? You are a child of God. Your playing small does not serve the world. There is nothing enlightened about shrinking so that other people won't feel insecure around you. We are all meant to shine, as children do. We were born to make manifest the glory of God that is within us. It's not just in some of us; it's in everyone. And as we let our own light shine, we unconsciously give other people permission to do the same. As we are liberated from our own fear, our presence automatically liberates others."
—MARIANNE WILLIAMSON

Endnotes

1. Today in the Word, September 18, 1993.
2. A woman with multiple personalities, sixteen of them, to be exact, whose story was told in the 1970s through a book and film by the same name.

About the Author

BECKY HUNTER loves working alongside her husband, Joel, in ministry. The Hunters were married in Indiana in 1972 and served in the United Methodist Church there before becoming Central Florida residents in 1985—the year Dr. Hunter accepted the role of senior pastor of Northland, A Church Distributed.

As president of the Global Pastors Wives Network from 2006 through 2008, Becky led seminars on five continents and was featured in TIME magazine for her ministry to pastors' wives. She is the author of *Being Good to Your Husband on Purpose* and has been published in numerous Christian women's magazines.

Becky, a former high school biology teacher, and Joel are the parents of three sons: Joshua, Isaac, and Joel. Josh is married to Lisa. He is the CEO of Hunter Vision, a 3D LASIK provider in Orlando, Florida, where Joel is the founding ophthalmic surgeon. Joel is married to Elizabeth. Isaac, with his wife, Rhonda, founded Summit Church in Orlando, Florida in 2002. Isaac serves as the senior pastor.

Joel and Becky Hunter have six grandchildren: Noah, Jada, Ella, Lincoln, Luke, and Ava, who, at five years old, battled brain cancer for ten weeks and moved to Heaven on September 4, 2010.

Contact information:

Northland, A Church Distributed
530 Dog Track Road
Longwood, FL 32750
www.northlandchurch.net
407-949-4000
beckyhunter@whyher.org